Songs of Praise
Book of Prayer

For
Bob Campbell-Smith,
Gilleasbuig Macmillan
and Lucy Winkett,
who help me to pray.

SONGS OF PRAISE

Book of
Prayer

Andrew Barr

LION

A Lion Book
an imprint of
Lion Hudson plc
Wilkinson House, Jordan Hill Road,
Oxford OX2 8DR, England
www.lionhudson.com
ISBN 978 0 7459 5247 5

First edition 2007
10 9 8 7 6 5 4 3 2 1 0

By arrangement with the BBC

BBC logo © BBC 1996
Songs of Praise logo © BBC 2000

The BBC logo and *Songs of Praise* logo are
registered trademarks of the British Broadcasting
Corporation and are used under licence

A catalogue record for this book is available
from the British Library

Typeset in 11.5/14 ITC Berkeley Oldstyle
Printed and bound in Great Britain

Bible verse acknowledgments

p.19 Scripture quotations are from The Holy
Bible, English Standard Version, published by
HarperCollins Publishers, copyright (c) 2001
Crossway Bibles, a division of Good News
Publishers. Used by permission. All rights
reserved.

pp. 52, 65, 106, 107, 127 Scripture quotations
are from the New Revised Standard Version
published by HarperCollins Publishers,
copyright (c) 1989 by the Division of Christian
Education of the National Council of the
Churches of Christ in the USA, and are used by
permission. All rights reserved.

pp. 54, 98 Extracts from the Authorized Version
of the Bible (The King James Bible), the rights in
which are vested in the Crown, are reproduced
by permission of the Crown's Patentee,
Cambridge University Press.

Contents

Foreword

• • • • • • • • • • • • • • •

Songs of Praise Book of Prayer is a natural successor to previous books in a series in which the programme's audience joined the search for the nation's favourite hymns, carols and churches. Like its predecessors, this book aims to bring together the familiar with the less familiar. You will find here some prayers you may know by heart from childhood, others that were prayed by people whose way of life has been admired, and others that are new; I hope they will bring you comfort and hope as well as challenge you.

'Birds fly, fishes swim – and human beings pray' is how David Conner, Dean of Windsor, introduced the subject on a BBC Radio 4 *Sunday Service*. He continued, 'There is, deep down in each human being, some spiritual impulse and energy that is constantly yearning and aching and longing for a fuller life and a better world.'

This book describes how some of our most famous prayers came to be written down, sometimes more than a thousand years ago. There are stories of some surprising responses, including pitched battles and even wars, as people fought over their use. A legendary incident still draws visitors from around the world to St Giles' Cathedral in Edinburgh, where they ask to see the wooden stool that a woman named Jenny Geddes threw at Dean Hannay on 23 July 1637 as he tried to read morning prayers from a new book. Imposed by the Archbishop of Canterbury, this book of prayers was met with much opposition: the Earl of Montrose, a Covenanter, called it 'the brood of the bowels of the whore of Babylon'. It was said that the subsequent riots against King Charles I led to an outburst of national feeling as strong as that which had led the Scots into battle with the English at Bannockburn. We in Britain have an incredibly rich heritage, and a surprising amount of our story and culture can also be found in familiar prayers.

This *Book of Prayer* was compiled by listening to stories on *Songs of Praise*, by sharing prayers in church and, perhaps most of all, by noticing the hymns that really take off when they are sung. It has ended up as a snapshot of prayer rather than a 'top ten' list. The snapshot reveals how much traditional language still matters. Even though prayer and the experience of prayer have so often been at the heart of *Songs of Praise*, the chance to find out which prayers people value most sometimes met with an unexpected response.

'That's a very personal matter,' said one person who had, up to that moment, been full of stories. 'It's rather impertinent of you to think that I might tell you.' 'If I did believe in God, I wouldn't tell you,' said another. This sort of response became familiar as I travelled around. 'Look in the Bible,' another person chided me. '"Pray in secret... when you pray, go to a place on your own... tell no one" – isn't that what it says?'

Other people came up with even odder explanations for their inability to help me. 'I used to be Methodist, but now I'm nothing,' answered one regular *Songs of Praise* viewer mysteriously, having told me, while we were waiting for the recording to begin, that this was her last appearance in the congregation before major surgery. 'You should ask her,' she continued, nodding to her neighbour. 'She's Salvation Army, and a more regular viewer of *Songs of Praise*.' A man sitting in a church that he had served faithfully for years responded vehemently to my question about his favourite prayer: 'Don't put me down as good! I'd only be good if I came to church when I didn't want to.' One person sent me a long, long list of the people for whom she was praying that week, but declined to say which words helped her.

The choice of a 'favourite' prayer seemed to have been thought of as a test of character: it would make you sound overly pious to say you had one. Deep down, perhaps, as the Dean of Windsor says, most of us are not satisfied with who we are.

The Billy Taylor spiritual recorded by Nina Simone in 1967, and once used as a hymn in another Radio 4 *Sunday Service*, sums up a yearning:

> *I wish I knew how it would feel to be free;*
> *I wish I could break all the chains holding me.*
> *I wish I could say all the things that I should say*
> *Say 'em loud, say 'em clear*
> *For the whole round world to hear.*
> **'I wish I knew how it would feel to be free' by Billy Taylor (b.1921)**

Even now, when a story is told on *Songs of Praise* about putting into practice prayers of forgiveness, there is a big response from the audience, and sometimes even the cameraman may be in tears when the story ends. Such a response occurred when a Japanese woman appeared on a programme about peacemakers to talk about her work. More than sixty years after VJ Day marked the end of the Second World War, Keiko Holmes OBE persuades now elderly former British prisoners of war to travel to Japan with her to meet the young descendants of their original captors. Men, some of whom may have been eaten up with bitter hatred for years, discover in these meetings that they can now offer the words and gestures of forgiveness.

There is another side to prayer. Letters, telephone calls and emails from viewers and listeners continually show producers and broadcasters how important prayer, whether found in books, sung in hymns, or heard in broadcasts, still is in the lives of many people. I hope that you will find that your favourites have been included.

> *All who received the Word,*
> *by God were blessed,*
> *sisters and brothers they*
> *of earth's fondest guest.*

So did the Word of Grace
proclaim in time and space,
and with a human face,
'I am for you.'
'Before the world began' by John L. Bell (b. 1949)
and Graham Maule (b. 1958)

My thanks are due once again to Morag Reeve and Julie Frederick at Lion Hudson as well as Hugh Faupel, editor of *Songs of Praise*, and Ashley Peatfield, editor of faith programmes on the BBC's English local radio stations, who helped me in my search. Thanks are also due to my colleagues on the Joint Liturgical Group of the UK, who represent many Christian denominations in the writing of new prayers for the churches.

Andrew Barr
Pentecost 2007

Help!

• • • • • • • • • • • • •

From 'O God' to The Lord's Prayer

After the 7 July London bombings at least a couple of the tabloid newspapers filled the whole of their front page with just two words: O GOD. After any unexpected disaster – the crash, the deafening noise, the blinding flash, an assault on every sense – there follows an equally unexpected aftermath of stillness and silence. Then someone says, 'O God!'

I have heard the voice myself. I had a car accident forty years ago, on the way back from late-night work at the BBC. It could just have been a voice in my head, or the voice of the friend who was walking past the wreck and found me trapped: 'O God!'

Last year my wife Liz and I were driving south through a beautiful sunlit landscape, following a lorry carrying a vast rock weighing many tons. It looked a little unsteady and we thought of it suddenly tipping off the back and crashing onto us. We laughed. But I felt a little uneasy and so was driving warily, although I could never have predicted what was about to happen. As we turned a corner, the rock broke loose from its mooring and crashed down onto the road in front of us, rolling rapidly towards us. As it came nearer and nearer, time seemed suspended. The stone stopped – and so, just in time, did we. 'Jesus Christ!' I said.

Was my response a prayer or an oath? What we say in these moments of crisis seems to come from somewhere deep down. I really meant 'O thank you!' that I would live another day.

O God! Thy arm was there;
And not to us, but to thine arm alone,
Ascribe we all.
from *Henry V* by William Shakespeare (1564–1618)

Preparing to film a sequence for a BBC documentary about the fire service, I walked past a bus stop. A few yards on, I heard a great crash behind me. Turning round, I saw that a lorry had overturned and the bus stop had vanished under tons of timber planks. When I recovered from the shock, I could not remember whether anyone had been waiting at the stop. Neither could anyone else who came rushing out of their cars. 'Hello? Is anyone there?' and 'O God!' we chorused. The cry is always the same, even in our aggressively individualistic world.

Often strangers become neighbours through an unexpected disaster. The BBC's *News 24* television channel showed just such a moment in a news-clip that lasted less than thirty seconds. An amateur cameraman, filming a flash flood in Newcastle, caught the moment when a small car got stuck. As the water rose around it, the car began to roll over and float away. The driver's door opened and an elderly man could be seen struggling to escape. An unseen voice near the camera said, 'Oh no, someone's trapped!'

Two young men, who until then looked as if they might have been hanging around up to no good, dashed, fully clothed, into the water, swimming the last few feet to wrench the passenger door open and lift out the driver's wife. Endowed with youthful strength but also with evident tenderness, they carried her and her husband into the shallows near the pavement. As they began their journey to safety in the arms of these young men, the old couple reached out to hold each other's hands. 'Oh look, they're pensioners!' said the commentator. 'God bless them.'

The words of the prayer of the Revd Eli Jenkins, 'We are not wholly bad or good / Who live our lives under Milk Wood', seemed to me, watching the report, to fit the whole incident perfectly. Written by Dylan Thomas for his epic radio poem, *Under Milk Wood*, it was sung as an anthem by a Welsh male voice choir on *Songs of Praise* some years ago, the choice of Carla Lane. She is the creator of several popular television series, including *Bread*, a programme about the wayward Boswell family in Liverpool, supervised by a formidable matriarch – played by Jean Boht – who began every family meal with the firm command, 'Prayers, everybody.' Carla Lane is another writer whose characters, just like the rest of us, are neither wholly bad nor good, a sentiment echoed by Dylan Thomas:

> *Every morning when I wake,*
> *Dear Lord, a little prayer I make,*
> *O please to keep Thy lovely eye*
> *On all poor creatures born to die.*
>
> *And every evening at sun-down*
> *I ask a blessing on the town,*
> *For whether we last the night or no*
> *I'm sure is always touch-and-go.*
>
> *We are not wholly bad or good*
> *Who live our lives under Milk Wood,*
> *And Thou, I know, wilt be the first*
> *To see our best side, not our worst.*
>
> *O let us see another day!*
> *Bless us this night, I pray,*
> *And to the sun we all will bow*
> *And say, good-bye – but just for now*
> **from *Under Milk Wood* by Dylan Thomas (1914–53)**

When *Under Milk Wood* was performed in the Kent Parish where we lived for ten years, we all recognized ourselves and our neighbours in the characters. However, the producer did not cast Bob the vicar in the role of the Revd Eli Jenkins, but rather in the part of the sinister teacher, Mr Pugh, who spends his spare time concocting poisonous cocktails for his overbearing wife. While there was not a scrap of truth of this in the vicarage, the part was played with huge relish by Bob.

In reality Bob was very similar to the Revd Eli Jenkins, and cared for the souls of everyone in the village not from a lofty pedestal of sanctity, but by walking with us and sharing the rhythm of our lives; he completely understood how all of us were 'not wholly bad or good'. Whether Bob was absailing in terror down from the top of the church tower for charity, or holding the hand of a dying person, he was also a man in a muddle who regularly announced the wrong hymn, left his sermon/microphone/communion chalice behind in the vestry, and on one occasion arranged for a group of us to bed down in a roomful of rats, mosquitoes and cockroaches in the middle of the Sri Lankan jungle. Bob also knew that even the most incorrigible 'Nogood Boyo' wanted to be 'Good Boyo' deep down.

Twenty years before Dylan Thomas' fictional Revd Eli Jenkins was heard on the radio – incidentally played by the playwright himself – another, real priest was trying to show people how to pray on the difficult road of life, and also through the medium of wireless:

For us, as for Christ, there is only one way to meet our perplexities and crosses: We must go right up to them and confront them in the name of God the Father, God the Son, and God the Holy Spirit, until they fly, as ultimately they will, from the wrath of God.
from a sermon by the Revd Dick Sheppard, broadcast in summer 1934

If prayer can be the heartfelt, involuntary cry of 'O God', even from people who never go to church, then there is another prayer that Christians say all around the world, in every language, in churches, in homes, on mountains, at sea – even in the jungle surrounded by cockroaches. This prayer is not a sudden cry of alarm or despair, but a preparation for each day in an uncertain world. Experiences often described on *Songs of Praise*, in war and in peace, in ugly cities and in beautiful landscapes, show that everyone who follows Jesus must learn to love their enemies, to forgive them and to turn the other cheek when attacked. Here, in this short prayer, is the upside-down world of the Christian faith: Jesus taught us to move from the instinct of self-preservation, to put others' needs before our own, and to have faith in the future:

> *Our Father, who art in heaven,*
> *hallowed be thy name;*
> *thy kingdom come;*
> *thy will be done;*
> *on earth as it is in heaven.*
> *Give us this day our daily bread.*
> *And forgive us our trespasses,*
> *as we forgive those who trespass against us.*
> *And lead us not into temptation;*
> *but deliver us from evil;*
> *For Thine is the kingdom,*
> *the power and the glory,*
> *for ever and ever.*
> *Amen.*

The Lord's Prayer, from *The Book of Common Prayer* (1662)

Creation

● ● ● ● ● ● ● ● ● ● ● ● ● ●

The rhythm of life

Sun and moon, bow down before him;
Dwellers all in time and space.
from 'Praise my soul, the King of heaven' by H.F. Lyte (1793–1847)

One night, driving home through the winter countryside, I saw a strange light in the east – particularly strange since it was coming from an area where I knew there was no town. The light rimmed a large hill called Traprain Law, the remains of an ancient volcano where there had once been a settlement. First inhabited in 1500 BC, the long-abandoned city was built by a Celtic tribe that the Romans, invading Britain in the time of Christ, called the Votadini. Precious relics are still being unearthed on the uninhabited hillside.

I received a second shock when a huge white disc rose rapidly up behind the hill. For a second I even began to imagine I was seeing my first UFO, so it was a relief to realize that it was nothing more than the full moon in flight. In an earlier, less scientific, less 'knowing' age, people were in awe of this weird apparition in the sky. Even on that December night it seemed magical enough to me and, after the first shock, a beautiful and holy moment, an encouragement to prayer.

Soon as the evening shades prevail,
The moon takes up the wondrous tale,

And nightly to the listening earth
Repeats the story of her birth;
While all the stars that round her burn,
And all the planets in their turn,
Confirm the tidings as they roll,
And spread the truth from pole to pole.
based on Psalm 19, Joseph Addison (1672–1719)

Joseph Addison, writer and Member of Parliament in the eighteenth century, found his inspiration for the hymn 'The Spacious Firmament on high' from this image of the moon rising over the landscape, illustrating the words of the psalmist, 'The heavens are telling the glory of God' (Psalm 19:1). In his day, philosophers and theologians wrote a great deal about the natural world. Nature was a resource 'designed for the being and service and contemplation of man', as preached an Anglican vicar of the time.

But earlier, seventeenth-century thinkers thought quite otherwise, and their gloomy meditations sound more like the predictions made today about global warming. 'Both the ages of man and the nature of all things time hath changed – and changed for the worse', wrote the courtier and explorer, Sir Walter Ralegh in 1614. The philosopher and Church of Scotland minister of Govan, Hugh Binning, prefaced his prayers gloomily: 'This is the world's old age... the truth is, and a believer knows, it is near the grave. The creation now is an old rotten house that is all dropping through.' At this time, London was polluted with the smoke of thousands of coal fires. One citizen wrote, 'We live in a kind of twilight, a cloudy and foggy clime of sadness and uncertainty.'

Even the heavens were thought to be full of ominous signs. During the English Civil War, people claimed to see apocalyptic battles in the sky with angels and demons in combat among banks of storm clouds. The world was growing old, man's sin had wrecked it, and the end was nigh.

Oh Lord God, look upon us in mercy, it is an evil time.
Bring good out of all these troubles and fears for the Lord's sake.
Robert Woodford, Puritan lawyer and diarist

In the more optimistic eighteenth century, Joseph Addison thought that God had made the best arguments for his own existence in the formation of the heavens and the earth, and that 'any man of sense' escaping from the 'hurry and noise of human affairs' would be convinced. People interviewed these days on *Songs of Praise* have often said that a walk in the countryside is as good as going to church.

My late father-in-law, Harold, who was not a churchgoer, still always sat and listened to the whole of Handel's *Messiah* on 78 rpm records every Christmas Eve. 'I thought I saw all heaven before me, and the great God himself,' wrote Handel, describing his own feelings as he composed the great choral masterpiece. One spring day, as Harold walked into the field at the bottom of his garden, he envisioned a great avenue of chestnut trees leading up to the family home – his own wordless prayer of thankfulness for the creation. Last summer I saw something that he never saw in his own lifetime. In the middle of the field stands the one and only tree he ever actually planted more than forty summers ago, now with a huge trunk. Beneath its wide branches a little flock of sheep were lying peacefully asleep, safely protected by his tree from the fierce sun.

Slow me down, Lord!
Ease the pounding of my heart by the quietening of my mind.
Steady my hurried pace with a vision of the eternal reach of time.
Give me the calmness of the everlasting hills.
Break the tensions of my nerves and muscles with the soothing music
Of the singing stream.
Help me to know the magical restoring power of sleep.
Teach me the art of taking minute vacations…

Of slowing down to look at a flower, to chat with a friend, to pat the dog,
To read a few lines from a good book.
Remind me each day of the fable of the tortoise and the hare,
That I may know that the race is not always to the swift:
That there is more to life than measuring its speed.
Let me look upwards into branches of the towering oak
And know that it grew great and strong
Because it grew slowly and well.
Slow me down, Lord, and inspire me
To send my roots deep into the soil of life's enduring values
That I may grow towards the star of my greatest destiny.
from *Short Prayers for the Long Day* (1996)
by Giles and Melville Harcourt

———

People still sometimes fear it is the judgement of God when nature turns hostile and our lives are in peril, as happened in the south of England one night in the autumn of 1987, soon after BBC weatherman Michael Fish told us all not to worry about an approaching storm. Liz was staying with her parents in London, and I was alone with the cat in our small medieval wooden house in Kent. As the whole building started to shudder, the night sky became blinding white with lightning flashes, but there was no thunder. Soon the house was being attacked by a violent wind that threatened to flatten everything in its path. It was like a great battle scene, and as I lay rigid in my bed, I could hear the approaching roar of each assault. Garden sheds and small trees turned into terrifying missiles flying through the air. Then an eerie silence would descend before the next wave.

I was still awake at two o'clock in the morning when, with one final enormous flash lighting up the whole Weald, all the electric lights went out. Not until the clouds were blown away an hour or so later could I see that the sky and a few stars were still in place. Vaguely reassured that the world had not ended, I fell asleep at last, wondering how the church and the vicarage had fared, and remembering the vicar's habit of saying 'fear not' whenever I worried about some minor matter. I tried to concentrate on a verse of scripture we had studied on the Kent local radio Lent course earlier that year, which I had had some difficulty believing:

Jesus answered them… 'Therefore I tell you, whatever you ask for in prayer, believe that you have received it, and it will be yours'
Mark 11:24

When morning came, the world had fallen silent. Amazingly, our little medieval home was completely intact. The brick gable of a nearby modern house was scattered all over the road among the fallen trees and torn up fences. The wind still lurked over the hill and attacked me as I struggled to open my front gate. The whole village was covered in debris, and a few bewildered neighbours were wandering about, wondering how to begin to clear up.

My first worry was about what had happened to Liz's two elderly donkeys in their field half a mile away. Half an hour later, having clambered over several fallen trees, I found them grazing quietly in their field in the light of the rising sun. They seemed unconcerned that their wooden shed, complete with bales of hay and straw, had blown several yards down the hill. The birds were singing, and although every autumn leaf had flown, their world seemed at peace.

Thankfully, in our village – although unfortunately not everywhere – we were all safe. The shared work of tidying up created many new friendships, and nature staged a most remarkable recovery, too. Although the seven oaks that gave the name to our nearby west Kent town had been reduced to one oak, the landscape all around us recovered its beauty without needing too much help from us, and there was never a better Easter in our part of the world than in 1988.

Oh Christ, who drives the furrow straight,
Oh Christ, the plough, Oh Christ, the laughter
Of holy birds flying after,
Lo, all my heart's field red and torn...
And Thou wilt bring the young green corn
The young green corn divinely springing,
The young green corn for ever singing;...
The corn that makes the holy bread
By which the soul of man is fed
The holy bread, the food unpriced,
Thy everlasting mercy, Christ.
The Everlasting Mercy by John Masefield (1878–1967)

Many times in Britain a storm of the night quietens and clears away as dawn breaks. Creation seems to be in a new mood and so, often, am I – in a new mood with a guest who had kept me up arguing far into the night, or with the cat who preferred jumping about in the cold, wet darkness to coming in so that the house could be locked up and we could all go to bed, or with a piece of work that just would not come right. A new day dawns. The line 'Morning by morning new mercies I see' from the hymn 'Great is thy faithfulness' often comes into my mind. Though I am not given to reciting hymns as I get dressed, this one has particular significance to me from my years of directing *Songs of Praise*, when I would hope that at least during this line the singers would remember to lift their heads out of their hymnals and show in their faces how often these good moments do happen.

Recently, finishing a film for the BBC, I woke up in the producer's house after a rather tetchy evening of editing. The morning sun was shining through the curtains, but it was the sights and sounds around me that really made my day begin well. Bethan, the Jack Russell, was whistling excitedly before going into the garden with Jack, the Labrador. George, the parrot, is always at his most talkative first thing. 'Morning, Peter,' he says to everyone who comes down for breakfast. Morse and Miss Marple, two young pure white cats, were proving that they had earned the right to be named after famous detectives as they barged in and searched through my luggage, having unlatched the bedroom door by themselves. Outside, donkeys and ponies were grazing, and repairs to their shelter revealed that Colin, the long-eared bat, had woken briefly from hibernation.

The world was at peace and the only person missing was St Francis. The twelfth-century merchant from Assisi claimed to have awakened one morning 'in great joy' to begin a journey to a life of simple poverty, one in which he found great companionship with all the animals. The night he died, larks came swooping low and singing over the house where he lay. Another of his Franciscan brothers saw his soul 'like a star ascending to heaven, having the immensity of the moon and the brightness of the sun'.

> *All creatures of our God and King,*
> *Lift up your voice and with us sing,*
> *alleluia, alleluia!*
> *Thou burning sun with golden beam,*
> *thou silver moon with softer gleam:*
> *O praise him, O praise him,*
> *alleluia, alleluia, alleluia!*
>
> **from 'All creatures of our God and King'**
> **after St Francis of Assisi (1182–1226)**

Prayer and Broadcasting

● ● ● ● ● ● ● ● ● ● ● ● ●

Courage and divine common sense

Holy Father, please do in me,
with me and through me: What You Want.
A prayer used at the first broadcast services from
St Martin-in-the-Fields by Revd Pat McCormick (1877–1940)

'I can hear his voice now, always beginning his prayer with the words "Holy Father".'

Now in her nineties, Patricia Frank has vivid memories of something I would love to have experienced – hearing her father, Revd Pat McCormick, together with the famous radio padre, Dick Sheppard, leading some of the earliest services broadcast on the radio from St Martin-in-the-Fields, the church in Trafalgar Square near the BBC's then studio at Savoy Hill.

Patricia still remembers the moments leading up to a 'live' broadcast from St Martin's. First Dick Sheppard himself would rehearse the hymns with the whole congregation, often a week earlier, just as *Songs of Praise* still prepares the congregations today. The church would be jammed with people standing in the aisles and sitting on the altar rail. People even sat on the steps up to the pulpit; the preacher was completely surrounded. Just before a light went on at his side to show that they were 'on the air', Dick Sheppard would ask everyone to pray in their own heart for 'the job that they were doing for thousands and thousands of listeners throughout the world'. For Patricia, even as a young child watching from the vicarage pew in the gallery, 'there was love in the whole experience'.

Her memories rewind history back to the 1920s, when the world was still reeling from the catastrophic loss of life in the First World War. Missing sons, brothers, fathers, husbands and boyfriends had created a nation of grieving women and children. Many turned to séances and spiritualist meetings, desperate to find out what had happened to the thousands who were listed 'missing, presumed dead'. Men who had survived came home wondering where God had been during all the carnage they had endured. Friends and comrades had been obliterated, and they grieved, but also felt strangely guilty for having survived themselves.

Dick Sheppard, the vicar of St Martin-in-the-Fields, had been with the troops in the trenches. His church was always open to the war-weary and the grief-stricken. Whenever he spoke from the pulpit, people felt he identified with them, and they with him. Thousands queued to get into his church to hear him preach.

Patricia's father, Pat McCormick, was a natural choice to join him and 'come to the microphone', as the early broadcasts were described. He too had gone to the Front, in 1914, as a chaplain. He conducted one service in a gun shelter near the trenches, where the roof was too low for the preacher to stand and where he had prayed and preached on the theme 'He thanked God and took courage'. Just before the battle, a few yards from the Front, fifty men received communion from him.

> *And when he giveth the cup to any one, he shall say*
> *'The Body of our Lord Jesus Christ, which was given for thee,*
> *Preserve thy body and soul unto everlasting life.*
> *Take and eat this in remembrance that Christ died for thee,*
> *And feed on him in thy heart by faith with thanksgiving.'*
> **The Book of Common Prayer** (1662)

However, the communion service itself, which had been all important for so many soldiers in the trenches, was not broadcast over the air at all in those early days. It was not for the obvious reason – that the bread and the wine could not be delivered by radio – but because to John Reith, the BBC's first director-general, Holy Communion and indeed all the sacraments were a matter of controversy between the churches; they created division. Under the BBC's first agreement with the government, nothing of any sort that was controversial was to be broadcast. Many aspects of church doctrine and practice fell under a ban that was intended to stop the secular political trouble-makers of the time, but in those days, prayer was regarded as just as dangerous as politics.

John Reith was fortunate with one of his tasks – that of providing religious programmes – to have come across Dick Sheppard. The vicar agreed when Reith defined the shape and tone of BBC religious programmes as 'upright, manly, thorough-going and utterly without controversy'. It was to be 'good talk' delivered by a believer with common sense. The first broadcasts were sermons of the sort that had brought so many people into St Martin-in-the-Fields, delivered by speakers of conviction who had experienced suffering and war at first hand.

To begin with, to avoid controversy, the Bible was not to be read, nor the traditional prayers of the churches heard, and even the hymns were chosen with extreme caution in case they could be used for doctrinal point-scoring. Fortunately, Sheppard and McCormick, together with a small band of others, were all extraordinarily gifted in their ability to sense the needs of the new medium and the circumstances of the unseen listener. Their words wrapped up the experiences of exhortation, prayer and praise without any hint of the divisions that afflicted, and still afflict, individual churches – and which, it has to be said, have been fought over through a thousand years of British history.

*O God whose never-failing providence ordereth all things in heaven and
     earth,*

*bless we beseech Thee all those who have the responsibility of directing the
affairs of this British Broadcasting Corporation with courage and divine
     common sense*

so that listeners may receive real re-creation of mind and spirit,

*and truth may flourish in our land, and go forth unto the ends of the
     world.*

Inspire all who will speak or sing or play with noble ideals,

*that they may give of their best whether grave or gay, instructive or
     humorous,*

and all may feel it is filling a real purpose in life for the common good.

We ask it through Jesus Christ our Lord.

**A prayer from the first Daily Service, transmitted from
the new 'religious' studio in Broadcasting House in 1932**

This prayer of dedication was written by Revd Hugh Johnston, another of
the clergy based at St Martin-in-the-Fields. He took the very first *Daily
Service*, a programme that began life as a service from a studio in 1928 and
is still broadcast live from a church every weekday on BBC Radio 4. Early
in 1932 the *Daily Service* moved into its own elegant studio in the new
Broadcasting House in London. The singers sat round a dining-room table
to perform, while the speaker would sit facing an alcove onto which the
outline of the cross was projected.

Hugh Johnston's prayer gives us a rare insight into the type of prayer
that would have been heard on the BBC before recordings were made. To
me, it has not dated much, and in a recent broadcast of the *Daily Service*,
the Revd Stephen Shipley, BBC producer of many radio services, who
continues the custom of writing his own prayers, echoes many of the same
themes. As in 1932, the prayers we hear over the air today can become
our own:

Work within me, Lord, within us, within the church,
be at the centre of our lives.
Mould us in your image.
Bring about our transformation.
Make us effective, Lord, now, here as well as there, me as well as others.

And we pray for each other.
Fill us with praise for all you have given us through our friendships.
Shield us in all our relationships from hasty words and disregard of truth.

Strengthen us in prayer
so that our lives may be sustained by your continual presence.
The Revd Stephen Shipley

———

John Reith grew up in a Glasgow manse at the end of Queen Victoria's reign. He was the youngest of seven, by a long way, and had a lonely childhood. His father, Dr George Reith, was a quiet and distant figure, greatly loved by the congregation of the College Church. Life in the manse, which John Reith in later years summed up as a place of 'ground rice and sago pudding', was austere, but George Reith was liberal in his beliefs and, unusually for a Presbyterian, had a painting in his study of the Roman Catholic cardinal, John Newman (author of the hymn 'Lead kindly light'). George Reith was apparently a caring man and preached at great length from John's Gospel on love, but for some reason he seems to have found little time to give affection to his youngest child at home.

Reith idolized his remote father and, after a difficult time at school, set out to match him. He took on challenges, initially in the First World War trenches, where he took great risks with enormous courage, and later, from 1922, in the Herculean task of quite literally 'inventing the BBC'.

Three years earlier, as his father lay dying, he had said to his son, 'Without me, you can do nothing.' Was he quoting the words of Jesus, or was he declaring disappointment in his son? Whatever he meant, it seems to have caused John Reith to set himself a ferocious agenda. He believed that radio-listening at home could unite a disorderly and immoral population. Radio was directed by one man seated in a London office controlling 'a machine that fashions the thoughts, colours the mind, governs the outlook and sways the emotions of millions of people'.

He was always to be disappointed by the results of his work and – even though he became Lord Reith – by the absence of proper recognition. He left the BBC hoping to be appointed Viceroy of India, which was not to be, and even at age eighty he was still praying that God might yet 'have some tremendous work for me to do'.

Although Reith often led and made extempore prayer, even at his own wedding reception, he never recorded any of his own prayers in his prodigious diaries. Barbara Hickman, one of Reith's last secretaries, still treasures perhaps the only prayer in John Reith's own handwriting in existence. He wrote it out for her, placing it on her desk without further comment the day after her father died. It is likely that this was a prayer that Lord Reith had heard his own father pray after a death, perhaps in family prayers at home. It was probably George Reith's own extempore prayer, spoken not from memory but from the heart, and later always remembered as a source of comfort by his son:

O God, we remember before thee
all who have faithfully lived,
and all who have peacefully passed on into the unseen world.
We leave them in thy gracious keeping.
May we have the assurance of our continued fellowship with them in thee,
and realize that though converse be no longer possible according to the
* flesh,*
there is no separation in the realm of love.

Lift us into that light and love, where the church on earth
is one with the church in paradise.
A prayer known to John Reith,
first director-general of the BBC (1889–1971)

'John Reith gave the BBC its Old Testament,' says the current director-general, Mark Thompson, himself a committed Christian who once worked in the BBC's religious broadcasting department, as if this comparatively new industry, less than 100 years old, might somehow have its roots in centuries past.

During his solitary youth, John Reith seems to have become convinced that God had created him to be a latter-day Moses. As he walked back home to the manse, he would look across to the north to the Campsie Hills, hoping to hear in the wind that gusted across the city a message for him from those hills. As a child, he had climbed in the Cairngorm Mountains of the Highlands with his father; after George Reith died, his son wrote that he hoped one day to ascend the mountain again and find his beloved father waiting for him up in the clouds.

Today, John Reith's ashes lie buried by the wall of a ruined church deep in the forest of Rothiemurchus in Inverness-shire. Above are the snow-capped mountains he loved. When Barbara Hickman was interviewed by 'Lord John', her future employer, he asked her not about her shorthand and typing skills, but whether she knew the Scottish metrical paraphrase 'Behold! the mountain of the Lord'. She did, and was able to sing it to the satisfaction of her new boss, and so begin work.

Behold! the mountain of the Lord
In latter days shall rise
On mountain tops above the hills,
And draw the wondering eyes.
from Scottish Paraphrases (1781), based on Isaiah 2:2–5

The Church Diary

• • • • • • • • • • • • •

The Christian year

The church and BBC's religious programmes begin their renewed spiritual journey not on 1 January, but at the end of November. As the hours of daylight shorten and the calendar year comes to an end, the church's new year begins on Advent Sunday:

> *Almighty God, give us grace that we may cast away the works of*
> *   darkness,*
> *and put upon us the armour of light,*
> *now in the time of this mortal life,*
> *in which thy Son Jesus Christ came to visit us in great humility;*
> *that in the last day, when he shall come again in his glorious Majesty,*
> *to judge both the quick and the dead,*
> *we may rise to the life immortal;*
> *through him who liveth and reigneth with thee*
> *and the Holy Spirit, now and ever. Amen.*
> **Collect for the first Sunday in Advent,**
> **from *The Book of Common Prayer* (1662)**

For the four Sundays of Advent, the prayers of the church reflect a season of preparation for the news of the birth of Jesus on Christmas Day. In Britain, the birds have fallen silent, and the commonest sounds are those of office parties and of crowds doing their frenzied Christmas shopping. It is not the easiest time for Christians to slow down and spend their days in quiet contemplation, but this is what we pray for. One little bird, who each year winters far away in Africa, will not delay long before he sets off on his long journey back to us, and will arrive in the new light of spring:

> *O come, O come, thou swallow small,*
> *Responding to your infants' call,*
> *Fly far and wide across the earth*
> *And end with hope our winter's dearth.*
> *Rejoice! Rejoice! A tiny bird*
> *Shall show a truth that seems absurd.*
> **from *Expectant: Verses for Advent* by Jim Cotter**

When Christmas Eve arrives at last, everyone crowds into churches and cathedrals in their thousands. They come from all directions – some in cars, some walking and carrying torches, some yawning, some, it has to be said, a little tiddly from an evening spent in the pub, and many who have not appeared since last Christmas Eve and will not be seen there again until the next one. All are happy to be coming together to celebrate Christmas at midnight with carols, readings and prayers, and all are welcomed.

> *O Holy Child of Bethlehem,*
> *Descend to us, we pray;*
> *Cast out our sin, and enter in,*
> *Be born in us today.*
> *We hear the Christmas angels*
> *The great glad tidings tell:*
> *O come to us, abide with us,*
> *Our Lord Emmanuel!*
> **from 'O little town of Bethlehem' by Phillips Brooks (1835–93)**

In Epiphany, the dark weeks of winter between Christmas and the beginning of Lent, the church celebrates the coming of the light of Christ into our dark world, and the coming of the wise men from the East, following a star. The wise men were to spread the news of what they had found in a stable in Bethlehem to men and women all over the world:

> And now we give you thanks
> because, in the incarnation of the Word,
> a new light has dawned upon the world,
> that all the nations may be brought out of darkness
> to see the radiance of your glory.
> **from *Common Worship* (2000)**

Just as the evenings begin to close in a little later each day and the first signs of spring appear in the garden, usually in March, the forty days of Lent begin. Shrove Tuesday is the last day for self-indulgence before Christians traditionally begin their long period of fasting and self-examination, in imitation of the forty days Jesus spent in the wilderness. On the day following Shrove Tuesday, Ash Wednesday, Christians in some churches have the sign of the cross marked on their foreheads in ash as a sign of penitence. This collect is said every day in Lent:

> Almighty and everlasting God,
> Who hatest nothing that thou hast made
> And dost forgive the sins of all them that are penitent:
> Create and make in us new and contrite hearts
> That we, worthily lamenting our sins
> And acknowledging our wretchedness,
> May obtain of thee, the God of all mercy,
> Perfect remission and forgiveness;
> Through Jesus Christ our Lord,

Who liveth and reigneth with thee,
In the unity of the Holy Spirit,
One God, now and forever.
The Collect for Lent first prayed on Ash Wednesday,
from *Common Worship* (2000)

Towards the end of Lent, on Palm Sunday, hymns and prayers tell the story of the few days when cheering crowds welcoming Jesus into Jerusalem on a donkey were changed into an angry mob demanding his death and watching him carry his cross to Calvary.

Ride on! Ride on in majesty!
Hark, all the tribes hosanna cry;
Thy humble beast pursues his road
With palms and scattered garments strowed.
from 'Ride on! Ride on in majesty!' by H.H. Milman (1791–1868)

Almighty God, we beseech thee graciously to behold this thy family,
For which our Lord Jesus Christ was content to be betrayed,
And given up into the hands of wicked men,
And to suffer death upon the cross,
Who now liveth and reigneth with thee and the Holy Ghost,
Ever one God,
World without end. Amen.
The Collect for Good Friday,
from *The Book of Common Prayer* (1662)

On Easter Sunday, the church celebrates the resurrection. This Easter prayer is also said in many churches daily throughout the year:

Jesus Christ is Lord.
Lord by your Cross and Resurrection

You have set us free.
You are the Saviour of the world.
The Acclamation of Faith, from *Common Worship* (2000)

By Whit Sunday the little swallows have returned and the trees are in leaf. On this day, the church remembers that, after Jesus had ascended into heaven, on the day of Pentecost, the apostles publicly received the gift and power of the Holy Spirit. This is the birthday of the church.

Almighty God,
who on the day of Pentecost
sent your Holy Spirit to the apostles
with the wind from heaven and in tongues of flame,
filling them with joy and boldness to preach the Gospel:
By the power of the same Spirit
strengthen us to witness to your truth
and to draw everyone to the fire of your love;
through Jesus Christ our Lord.
Collect for Whit Sunday, from *The Book of Common Prayer*
***of the Church of Ireland* (2004)**

Sometimes it is surprising how much the cycle of church festivals, feast days and fast days chimes with the moods, needs and experiences of daily life. We do not have to make it fit – it just does fit. After Pentecost comes the long summer and autumn of the twenty-six Sundays after Trinity.

Ex Deo nascimur – We are born from God
In Christo morimur – We die in Christ
Per Spiritum Sanctum reviviscimus – We are reborn through the Holy
   Spirit
A Latin Trinity, inscribed as an epitaph
on an ancient tomb in Germany

Everyone has a favourite prayer, and as we once more come round to the start of Advent and the church's new year, this is the one that most people who were asked to memorize a prayer every week at school seem to remember for the rest of their lives:

> *Stir up, we beseech thee, O Lord, the wills of thy faithful people;*
> *that they, plenteously bringing forth the fruit of good works, may of thee*
> *be plenteously rewarded; through Jesus Christ our Lord. Amen*
>
> **Collect for the twenty-fifth Sunday after Trinity,**
> **from *The Book of Common Prayer* (1662)**

Children

· · · · · · · · · · · · · ·

Thank you for making me me

Come and join the celebration,
It's a very special day;
Come and share our jubilation
There's a new King born today!
from 'Come and join the celebration' by Valerie Collison (b. 1933)

Last Christmas, I was in Coventry for a carol service in the cathedral. The Dean of Coventry, John Irvine, began with a moving prayer:

Lord Jesus, born in Bethlehem,
We pray for the children of the Middle East
Who look up at night to see the same stars
On which you gazed with hope and wonder.
May all who share the same sky learn to share the same land.

Songs of Praise music adviser and conductor, Paul Leddington Wright, was in charge of the music. Coventry Cathedral is almost home for him, and it is where he conducted a spectacular programme in 2007. But for once there would be no worries or hold-ups caused by television technicians and cameras, because he was as near off-duty as he allowed himself to be. All he had to do was organize 150 very young musicians into an orderly orchestra. Then, he said, they would be ready to teach us, sitting in the nave, to 'Come and join the celebration'. He had already smiled beguilingly at us, asking if we could look a bit more alive and a bit less comatose. I now realized why this item in the Coventry Christmas Carol Service was headed 'Children's time', with an ominous note '*Everyone*'.

When *Songs of Praise* organized a poll to find the nation's favourite carols, the song 'Come and join the celebration' had soared up the chart at the beginning of the voting during the Christmas Big Sing at the Royal Albert Hall. But it was not in the programme, and not many more people had voted for it later. Like many others, I had never heard it until finally somebody kindly played it to me over the telephone on an out-of-tune piano. Still, perhaps it is not surprising that I was not particularly looking forward to this impromptu performance in Coventry.

To begin with, the task of organizing the junior band looked quite hopeless. Paul disappeared into the middle of a wildly enthusiastic would-be orchestra, his arms waving like a semaphore signaller. We cleared our throats and waited.

'Now,' said Paul, finally emerging triumphantly from a neat array of musicians, including many drummers already honing their skills. 'You haven't got any words on your programme; you're just going to have to learn them.'

Luckily he had with him the cathedral's boy and girl choristers and the choir of Sketchley Hill Primary School, who had won the 2006 *Songs of Praise* Junior Choir School Competition. They turned out to be enthusiastic teachers, but I do not think our choir in the nave was up to much. The small boy sitting in front of me had been left behind by his family when his brothers and sisters had gone off with their instruments. He had not shown much enthusiasm so far, and had covered his ears when we sang 'O come, all ye faithful'. (Was I that bad?) He had then pulled his hoodie right over his head and sunk to the floor.

When we all sang with the impromptu orchestra for the first time, the din was extraordinary. The percussion section obviously intended to give it their all. The second time, with Paul making 'ssshh' noises in their direction, we began to hear the words. The third time, the very last go, was 'the performance', and quite unexpectedly the small boy in front of me suddenly threw off his hoodie, stood up and sang the whole chorus word-perfect. He grinned in celebration.

Dear God,
I have tried my best to be a good boy.
Sometimes I could try harder.
I promise to do my best and be nice to other people.
Amen.

This prayer was one of several written by children and attached to a big painting in a little Roman Catholic church in Dorset. I am not sure what the colourful splashes of paint were intended to show, but the artist had been enthusiastic. He had certainly done 'his best', and was being nice to the visitor by adding an eye-catching offering to a rather plain church. What I liked is that I am sure that the prayer had really been written and prayed by a child: only children have the honesty to admit that it can be really difficult 'to be nice' to other people. God's help with this task is the only hope.

Television producers broadcasting a church service often think that it would be good to have prayers written and spoken by children. Sometimes this produces surprising results as a small person struggles to fight his way through a very long prayer full of difficult words that were clearly written by an adult. There is no lack of juvenile originality at the Episcopal Cathedral in Edinburgh. Every Sunday before the service finishes, the youngest children rejoin the congregation after Sunday school, bringing their drawings, paintings, models and prayers up to the provost, and we all listen to their explanations. Sometimes there are whisperers and sometimes there are wonderfully confident seven-year-olds, probably preachers of the future. In either case, it is evident that they are telling us what they themselves think, and not what someone else has written for them to say. They always get a big cheer and a round of applause. How far we have come from the days of the Reformation 450 years ago at, when the Scottish *Book of Discipline* ordered that 'common prayers be publicly made, that the children and rude persons be instructed in the chief points of religion, and that offences be corrected and punished'.

─────────

If I were a wiggly worm,
I'd thank you, Lord, that I could squirm.
And if I were a fuzzy wuzzy bear,
I'd thank you Lord, for my fuzzy wuzzy hair;
If I were a crocodile,
I'd thank you, Lord, for my great smile.
But I just thank you, Father, for making me me.

For you gave me a heart and you gave me a smile,
You gave me Jesus and you made me your child,
And I just thank you, Father, for making me me.
from 'The Butterfly Song' by Brian Howard

Any adult who has tried to sing along to this song doing the actions of a worm, a crocodile and a fuzzy bear will know it is something best left to the young. Once on some obscure training exercise on a BBC management course, I had been required to be both an elephant and a giraffe, and as a giraffe I had managed to collide with my elephant neighbour so forcefully that he had to be taken to hospital.

So I wisely declined to join in when it was sung at assembly during my visit to a primary school in the Scottish Borders in 1994 – a visit that was to make a deep impression on me. Although this school was not in a particularly deprived area, I could not help noticing how much help many of the children needed at lunchtime. At least one in three had never been taught to use a knife and fork until they came to school.

That morning they were doing a project about animals in the jungle, and were learning about efforts to save wild beasts. There are very few wild beasts in the Borders, but even after lunch the children were still talking enthusiastically about how they could help. In the afternoon, the head teacher introduced a guest. She was a young Scot called Lesley Bilinda from the missionary and relief organization, Tearfund. She began by explaining that her name, which was unusual for a Scot, was due to her being married to a pastor from Rwanda. She was back in Scotland because her husband had vanished in the civil war that had broken out when she was working there as a midwife. She had had to give up the search while the war raged, killing at least 800,000 people, but she told the children that she would be returning to Rwanda to continue her search for her husband.

The class listened intently, and when she paused and asked for questions, a boy immediately asked what her husband's Christian name was. When she said it was Charles, two little girls stood up and said, 'Mrs Bilinda, would you let us pray for you?'

As a result of this chance meeting, Lesley Bilinda's story of her search for her husband, and then for his murderers, was later told in a BBC Scotland film. Since then, she has written books and appeared on a BBC Two series with Archbishop Desmond Tutu called *Facing the Truth*, in which killers were confronted with the families of their victims. Lesley believes in forgiveness, but she says that she had nearly abandoned her faith that year we had met in the primary school. But so many people had prayed for her that she managed to keep going. 'Forgiveness is a journey,' she says. The primary school children had helped her a good way on that journey.

Father God, I wonder
How I managed to exist
Without the knowledge of your parenthood and your loving care.
But now I am your child,
I am adopted in your family, and I can never be alone
'cause, Father God, you're there beside me.

I will sing your praises,
I will sing your praises,
I will sing your praises,
for ever more.
'Father God, I wonder' by Ian Smale (b. 1950)

Night and Day

● ● ● ● ● ● ● ● ● ● ● ●

Dawn follows the darkest night

Lighten our darkness, we beseech thee, O Lord; and by thy great mercy
defend us from all perils and dangers of this night;
for the love of thy only Son, our Saviour, Jesus Christ. Amen.
The third Collect, for aid against all perils,
from The Book of Common Prayer (1662)

As the shadows begin to lengthen and the stumps are drawn, the village cricket team returns to their pavilion, and as long as we are still 'in love and charity' with the victors from the neighbouring village, we can all amble together to the church. Passing through the ancient door underneath the church tower, with its clock that has counted out the long, balmy summer afternoon, we are in time to hear a voice that, if we are fortunate, knows how to read Shakespearean English, as the old Church of England *Book of Common Prayer* Service of Evening Prayer begins:

> *Dearly beloved brethren, the Scripture moveth us in sundry places to*
> *acknowledge and confess our manifold sins and wickedness; and that we*
> *should not dissemble nor cloke them before the face of Almighty God our*
> *heavenly Father…*

Although not so common an experience as it would have been before the days of *Songs of Praise*, there are a few small country churches where these familiar words, used in summer and in winter, in war and in peace, are still said on Sunday evenings. For the years when I served as a churchwarden in such a church, the lay reader used to lead our worship. The summer sun poured in through the open doors as we stood scattered about the sixteenth-century nave, while he declaimed the lengthy opening sentences from the prayer book. The bell-ringers, whose ringing had summoned us, would watch us for a few moments from behind the ringing-chamber window high up at the west end, casting long shadows over the pews. Before we could declare our sins, they would be off home, and as we knelt, the sun would start to set, finally catching the altar by the time we were blessed on our way. For me, there is no service from *The Book of Common Prayer*, originally authorized in 1549, which has better stood the test of time. The weekly broadcasts on BBC Radio 3 from cathedrals have helped keep it alive, but the experience in a small church should not be missed.

There were no prayers being said on a summer's day when I went into Bemerton Church for the first time. But this tiny and not especially eye-catching building on a sharp bend in a busy, but narrow, village road is famous for the minister and poet who would have said Evensong here on countless occasions in the seventeenth century. George Herbert forsook a life as a royal courtier to take holy orders and came to this little church not far across the meadows from Salisbury Cathedral, where he stayed until his death in 1632. Here he wrote a poem that describes his gratitude to God at the end of the day:

> *Blest be the God of love,*
> *Who gave me eyes, and light, and power this day,*
> *Both to be busie, and to play.*
> *But much more blest be God above,*
> *Who gave me sight alone,*
> *Which to himself he did denie:*
> *For when he sees my waies, I dy:*

But I have got his sonne, and he hath none.
'Evensong' by George Herbert (1593–1632)

Sitting in Bemerton Church, it is not difficult to imagine Herbert kneeling in prayer. Unlike the distant voice floating down from the great cathedrals heard on BBC Radio 3 in beautiful stereo, his voice would have been close and more urgent. There was an uneasy peace in George Herbert's time, but older people would have remembered the violent days of battle between Roman Catholics and Protestants, often fought out in actual churches, and in 1605, the Gunpowder Plot. Before long there would be yet another long, dark night: civil war in England.

Today in Britain the night is not to be dreaded so much for fear of plots and battles, but it can be a time when anxieties surface and sleep is impossible. Ephrem Lash, an Orthodox priest living in Manchester, has translated an ancient prayer for those who fear the long, lonely hours of the night. Often the first birds will be waking to sing the dawn chorus before the insomniac drifts off at last into a deep sleep.

I shall be sheltered in the shadow of your wings and I shall sleep,
For you alone have made me dwell in hope.
Into your hands, Lord, I entrust my soul and body.
Bless me yourself and have mercy on me,
And grant me the grace of eternal life. Amen.
Archimandrite Ephrem Lash

In my travelling days, I often had to wake up with the dawn birds to ensure that I arrived in the car park at Waverley Station in Edinburgh before the opening words on BBC Radio 4's *Prayer for the Day*. It was not so odd a place to say my morning prayer because, for centuries, where now there are tracks and platforms and a bleak car park, there once stood the Collegiate Church of the Holy Trinity. Here, in a sumptuous building, which was taken apart for the first railway travellers, monks prayed at dusk:

Watch, dear Lord with those
Who wake or watch or weep tonight,
And give your angels charge over those who sleep.
Tend your sick ones,
O Lord Jesus Christ,
Rest your weary ones,
Bless your dying ones,
Soothe your suffering ones,
Shield your joyous ones,
And all for your love's sake.
Attributed to St Augustine (354–430)

In George Herbert's day, people went to bed when it got dark, and woke at first light. I must always remember to take his poem 'Mattens' to one of the church conferences I regularly attend, where I find myself starting the day at dawn:

I cannot ope mine eyes,
But thou art ready there to catch
My morning-soul and sacrifice:
Then we must needs for that day make a match.

My God, what is a heart?
Silver, or gold, or precious stone,
Or starre, or rainbow, or a part
Of all these things, or all of them in one?

My God, what is a heart,
That thou shouldst it so eye, and wooe,
Powring upon it all thy art,
As if thou hadst nothing els to do?

Indeed mans whole estate
Amounts (and richly) to serve thee:
He did not heav'n and earth create,
Yet studies them, not him by whom they be.

Teach me thy love to know;
That this new light, which now I see,
May both the work and workman show:
Then by a sunne-beam I will climbe to thee.
'Mattens' by George Herbert (1593–1632)

After a hard day's work at these conferences, ending with evening prayers in an ancient monastic institution, delegates ignore the good practice of the monks, who would have retired into the 'great silence' until the dawn. We always announce plans to go to bed early, but then talk far into the night. The next morning I can scarcely open my eyes as, one by one, we gather in silence for morning prayer:

O Lord, our heavenly Father, Almighty and everlasting God,
Who hast safely brought us to the beginning of this day;
Defend us in the same with thy mighty power;
and grant that this day we fall into no sin, neither run into any kind of
  danger;
but that all our doings may be ordered by thy governance,
to do always that is righteous in thy sight;
Through Jesus Christ our Lord. Amen
The third Collect for Grace, from *The Book of Common Prayer* (1662)

I heard the voice of Jesus say,
'I am this dark world's light;
look unto me, thy morn shall rise,
and all thy day be bright.'

I looked to Jesus, and I found
In him my star, my sun:
And in that light of life I'll walk,
Till travelling days are done.
from 'I heard the voice of Jesus say' by Horatio Bonar (1808–89)

Extempore Prayer

● ● ● ● ● ● ● ● ● ● ● ● ●

Praying with the Bible

In *Songs of Praise* from St Asaph's Cathedral in North Wales on St David's Day, 2007, Aled Jones was shown the very first Bible to be translated into Welsh. Looking through William Morgan's fragile pages from the sixteenth century, Aled was told by local historian Bobi Owen, 'Whatever the language, the light will come through.' Words of prayer and the images they conjure up can be a window into history. Here is a prayer written in the hard world of sixteenth-century Europe:

> *Almightie God, and moste merciful father,*
> *We humbly submit our selves and fall down before thy majesty,*
> *Beseeching thee from the bottom of our hearts,*
> *That this seed sown amongst us may take such deep root,*
> *That neither the burning heat of persecution cause it to wither,*
> *Neither the thorny cares of this life do choke it,*
> *But that as seed sown in good grounde, it may bring forth*
> *An hundred fold as thy heavenly wisdom hath appointed.*
> *And because we have need continually, to crave many things at thy hands,*
> *We humbly beseech thee to grant us thy holy spirit to direct our petitions,*
> *That they may proceed, as may be agreeable to thy most blessed will.*
> **Prayer of John Knox from the Morning Service,**
> **from the *Genevan Service Book* (1556)**

I was surprised when I discovered in a second-hand shop an old book of prayers written by the reformer John Knox. I had always assumed that Knox relied on 'extempore prayer' – speaking to God with whatever words or ideas from the Bible that the Holy Spirit put into his heart. The word 'extempore' (literally 'out of time') has been adopted by the church to mean 'inspired in the moment by God', but the actual dictionary definition – 'without preparation; casual; makeshift' – does not give rise to such great expectations.

The above prayer is the first part of a very long printed prayer written down by Knox. The Service of Morning Prayer in Knox's time would have begun with a sermon, followed by a very long period of intercessory prayer, starting with these words. Eventually the preacher would have summed up all the extempore prayers in the words of the Lord's Prayer.

The English *Book of Common Prayer* was also used in Scotland after 1560. Even in the 1970s, when I was first broadcasting services from the Church of Scotland, I noticed that although worship was proudly Scottish, extracts from formal English prayers would emerge in the middle of the extempore prayer of the Kirk minister. They would sometimes even begin with a still familiar prayer that originally belonged to the pre-Reformation Church:

> *O God, from whom all holy desires, all good counsels,*
> *and all just works do proceed,*
> *Give unto thy servants that peace which the world cannot give;*
> *That both our hearts may be set to obey thy commandments,*
> *And also that by thee we being defended from the fear of our enemies*
> *May pass our time in rest and quietness.*
> *Through Jesus Christ our Lord. Amen.*
> **from The Sarum Missal**

Many hymns and most prayers, including this one, are created from scripture passages. The phrase 'that peace which the world cannot give' is from John 14:27. Charles Wesley drew on thirty-eight different verses from both the Old and New Testaments for his hymn 'Love Divine, all loves excelling'. As children, both Charles and John Wesley were taught to read by their devout mother using only the Bible, and John Wesley was so immersed in scripture that he even wrote quite routine letters based on biblical phrases and ideas.

Working for five years as chairman of the Liturgy Committee for the Scottish Episcopal Church has helped me recognize how many phrases from the Bible lie behind familiar prayers. Any writing of liturgy always begins with Bible study. As a committee given the task of writing a new Service of Baptism and later a new Marriage Service, we spent much time worshipping and praying together before even a single sentence was written down. Invariably the first results of our efforts would be a service that would have lasted about two and a half hours. It seems that there is a natural instinct among church people to include everything that makes up Christian belief in every liturgy – and then repeat it at least three times. Modern congregations prefer greater brevity.

> ... *shewe thy great mercies upon these our brethren, which are persecuted, cast in prison, and daily condemned to death, for the testimony of thy truth. And though they be utterly destitute of all man's aid, yet let thy sweet comfort never depart from them: but so inflame their hearts, with thy holy spirit, that they may boldly and cheerfully abide such trial, as thy godly wisdom shall appoint...*
> **Prayer of John Knox from the Morning Service,**
> **from the *Genevan Service Book* (1556)**

In spite of John Knox's written prayers, there is still a tradition for the Reformed Church minister to lead worship with extempore prayer. His familiarity with scripture would have been put to a weekly test by his congregation in the days when they all came to church fresh from reading their family Bible. Where the church building had a gallery giving a good view of the preacher in the pulpit, at least one stern critic would always be seated there, one eye on the clock and the other ensuring that there were no concealed crib notes. Incidentally, the clock-watching did not indicate a desire for brevity, but rather the opposite. Elongation was the watchword in those days.

Extempore prayer could lead ministers into great trouble. In May 1857, a vicious dispute about the quality of one minister's prayers even reached the headlines of Scottish newspapers, and much column space was filled reporting an astonishing ten-hour debate about his extempore devotions. This minister, Mr Law, had been offered to the parish of Kilmacolm, and he had had a bad beginning as he was second choice. (Mr Russell, the first choice offered to the congregation by the patron of the church, was dismissed by 'many objections', his prayers being 'without fervour, and spoken in a pompous and theatrical style'.)

The second minister elect was instructed to take two services under the scrutiny of several learned professors. While 'the Divines', as the academics were called, were generally satisfied, the congregation, including the village blacksmith and several farmers, was not. They began a campaign of objections that went on for months, and finally was brought to the General Assembly of the Church of Scotland meeting in Edinburgh. The criticisms, delivered in the full glare of publicity, began with Mr Law's prayers, which witnesses protested were 'without method, and full of repetitions, and evinced great poverty of thought'; while his sermons 'partook of the character of rhapsody, being made up of vague and unconnected ideas, having a bewildering effect, clouding the obvious meaning of texts. His style was puerile and uninteresting; his words hurled forth in an impetuous stream.'

How the hapless Mr Law ever prayed aloud or preached again after such public denunciation is hard to imagine. The debate continued far into the night. At 2.30 a.m., the General Assembly finally delivered their solemn judgement. By 110 votes to 71, they pronounced that the congregation was correct in refusing to accept their new minister and his prayers. Mr Law vanished and was replaced by a Mr Leck, who was immediately rejected on the grounds that he had a speech impediment. Preliminary hearings took up twenty-seven days. In 1858, the General Assembly went through yet another debate, about the parish of Kilmacolm. This time they told the congregation to stop protesting, and to find more charity for their minister.

In the nineteenth century, the primitive Methodist preacher in training would be accompanied in the pulpit by his teacher, who would use an umbrella or a stick to poke him in the ankle if he began wandering off the point. These horror stories are from a distant past, but even in more recent times one minister I know felt so threatened whenever he had to pray in public that he would have a recurring nightmare of finding that the pulpit had no floor, and that he could only remain visible by clinging on to the top, which in his dream was always covered by barbed wire.

Although the sermons of ministers in training are still appraised by their peers behind closed doors, lay Christians as well as ministers are all now encouraged to find the confidence to pray aloud with others. Some people find it helpful in a prayer group to begin with one person reading a passage from the Bible. They then find their own words to thank God for blessings, and they pray and talk to one another about things that concern them. But for many, praying out loud in front of others is a major hurdle. One group of young people from a Roman Catholic and an Anglican church in our village in Kent, who were preparing for confirmation together, found the idea of saying personal prayers out loud in the group impossible. When no one dared speak, someone suggested that next time they would all put paper bags over their heads so they couldn't see one another. It was an instant success.

I, too, do not find it easy to pray aloud with other people. In a group, I study the floor intently during the pause while the leader looks around for someone to begin. It seems to make me feel at my most inarticulate and unspiritual. But one dark January Sunday in church, I heard a lesson from the letter of Paul to the Colossians read with such beauty and understanding by an elderly lady that, verse by verse, it immediately became my own prayer. In the long silence that followed, I muttered words of gratitude and, sentence by sentence, made a late New Year's resolution.

As God's chosen ones, holy and beloved, clothe yourselves with compassion, kindness, humility, meekness, and patience. Bear with one another and, if anyone has a complaint against another, forgive each other; just as the Lord has forgiven you, so you also must forgive. Above all, clothe yourselves with love, which binds everything together in perfect harmony. And let the peace of Christ rule in your hearts, to which indeed you were called in the one body. And be thankful. Let the word of Christ dwell in you richly; teach and admonish one another in all wisdom; and with gratitude in your hearts sing psalms, hymns, and spiritual songs to God. And whatever you do, in word or deed, do everything in the name of the Lord Jesus, giving thanks to God the Father through him.
Colossians 3:12–17

No one sang more enthusiastically (though tunelessly) than I the hymn that followed her reading.

> *We have a gospel to proclaim,*
> *Good news for all throughout the earth;*
> *The gospel of a Saviour's name:*
> *We sing his glory, tell his worth.*
> **from 'We have a gospel to proclaim' by Edward Burns (b. 1938)**

Prayers of Place

● ● ● ● ● ● ● ● ● ● ● ● ●

Candles, coffee and chanting

The French philosopher Simone Weil, whose life combined mysticism and practical care for others, described why finding a place for prayer seems to be so important, even for people like her, who would never find an answer to their needs by becoming church members. Living a life of prayer and self-denial, she was never baptized, but she longed for the roots, the sense of place and the destiny of the soul that defines Christian belief:

To be rooted is perhaps the most important need of the human soul. A human being has roots by real, active and natural participation in the life of a community, which preserves in living shape certain particular treasures of the past and certain particular expectations of the future.
from 'The Need for Roots' by Simone Weil

In the middle of the seventh century a monastery was founded by Cedd, a monk from Northumbria. He picked a remote place on the edge of the north York moors. The Venerable Bede, historian and chronicler of the Dark Ages, described the place Cedd chose for his community of prayer as 'amid some steep and remote hills which seemed better fitted for the haunts of robbers and the dens of wild beasts than for human habitation; so that as a verse in Isaiah says: In the habitation where once dragons lay, shall be grass with reeds and rushes' (Isaiah 35:7).

Cedd began work on the site by spending the whole forty days of Lent fasting and praying. He believed that his prayers must first purge away all associations of evil in that place before building could begin. Today, the result of his prayers is the little church at Lastingham on the edge of wild moorland. As Jonathan Edwards explained in a *Songs of Praise* from Chelmsford, Cedd also went on to set up a church on a remote part of the Essex marshes. Constant prayer and reading scripture were the main activities in Britain's earliest churches, which were usually either monasteries or hermitages, often set in remote places and sometimes built on abandoned Roman settlements or places once associated with pagan worship. So Cedd's choice was not so odd for his own time.

> *Out of the depths have I called unto thee, O Lord:*
> *Lord hear my voice.*
> **De profundis: Psalm 130:1–2**

Down in Devon, when I was first taken to the Church of St Mary the Virgin, Upton Hellions, I was quite sure that I would never find my way back home again. Although rather proud of my sense of direction, the journey to this church involved weaving through a maze of narrow lanes fringed by tall hedges that clung to the side of the car as we passed by. You could easily imagine yourself at the back of a medieval Rogationtide procession, following the ancient custom of blessing the crops. Without any passing places, it was a miracle that we never came face to face with a tractor. But suddenly the lane widened, and there, through a small lychgate, was the church. We were back in the modern world, searching for somewhere to park.

John Betjeman, in his *Pocket Guide to English Parish Churches*, neatly sums up St Mary's: 'Unsophisticated country church in deep country. Plastered and whitewashed interior (always a good start for a country church).' He describes the wooden wagon roof and the carved benches from the fifteenth century. And there, too, as we went in, was what

Betjeman calls 'a country-made monument' to a squire and his wife from what the tourist guide used to call 'good King Charles' Golden days'.

It is difficult to believe that anyone comes across Upton Hellions by chance or can hope to find it without a guide. Although a priest now comes out from Crediton to pray with the present generation who look after the church and find God there, it would appear that the marauders of the Reformation – and later of the English Civil War – searching out idolatry, never found it either. In an old history of Devon's churches, I can find only one reference: the parish priest in the Middle Ages was instructed to move the dedication festival to another Sunday because it interfered with the cycle of prayers for the season of Advent. Years later, in 1549, 'love of the old ways' prompted the people of Devonshire to refuse to use King Edward VI's Reformation prayer book, but Upton Hellions seems to have quietly carried on, oblivious of the rebellion that led to violence in the county and the siege of nearby Exeter.

After sunset every Easter Eve, certainly until 1548, the people of Upton Hellions would assemble in the dark church to pray with their priest as a huge candle was lit from a fire of dried kindling wood near the font (the official service book, the *Order of Sarum*, said the candle was to be 'at least 36 feet in height', but this must surely be wrong). By this new light, the resurrection of Jesus from the tomb on the first Easter day was proclaimed:

Now let the angelic host of heaven exult,
let the divine mysteries be celebrated with exultation,
and let the trumpet of salvation sound
for the victory of so great a King.

This is the night in which thou first madest our fathers, the children of Israel, whom thou leddest up out of Egypt, to pass through the Red Sea dry-shod.
This therefore is the night in which he cleared away the shades of sin by the pillar of light.

This is the night which, as at this day, sets apart from the vices of this world and from the darkness of sin, and restores to grace, and unites in sanctity the believers in Christ throughout the whole world.
from the *Exultet*, Sarum Rite (1526)

Every year in some Anglican and in all Roman Catholic churches, these old words are still used, and the tall paschal candle lit and solemnly carried through the congregation. In the Kentish village of Goudhurst, once my home, the Anglicans and Roman Catholics of the village come together for this service, in which they renew their baptismal vows in the new light of Easter.

It seems that the old *Exultet* is no longer proclaimed in Upton Hellions, but as we wandered about on that first visit, we had an experience of the miracle of light. The whole interior was transformed in an instant as the sun burst through the plain-glass mullioned windows of the south aisle. The late poet Ruth Pitter described her response to a similar experience in a BBC Radio talk:

Suddenly, heaven blazed on me. I was enveloped in golden light, I was conscious of a presence, so kind, so loving, so bright, so consoling, so commanding, existing apart from me, but so close. I heard no sound. But words fell into my mind quite clearly – 'Everything is all right. Everybody will be all right.'

———

'Coffee and quiet' had been going for two hours, and Norman Wallwork, Methodist minister of Dursley, Cam and Wootton-under-Edge, encouraged me to break into a run as we approached Cam Chapel. 'We can't miss this,' he called over his shoulder.

We were welcomed into the little entrance hall of the Wesleyan chapel built in 1825 to serve a growing working population in Gloucestershire. Fresh coffee had just been brewed, even though it was really time for Joan and Jill to close the door. Their 'quiet place' coffee mornings had begun with a regular prayer meeting on Saturdays. Some people had popped in from the street because of the smell of the coffee; now the door is opened on weekdays, and all sorts of people come in to find something more than coffee. I discovered that 'popping in' is a Cam Chapel tradition. One person agreed to run the Sunday School for a few weeks, and did it for eighteen years. Another came to a Good Friday service in 1967, from their home miles away, and has never left. 'This is where God wants us,' said another.

There was nothing organized, but there were chairs so people could sit and chat over a cup of coffee, and an unofficial post box on the wall, used for messages that are sorted and delivered to people who cannot get to worship. Two frosted-glass doors behind us led to the heart of the building, a quiet place where people can sit alone in the simple little chapel. Closing the door behind me, I could no longer hear the street or the friendly conversation in the entrance hall. 'Quiet' turned into 'peace' as I sat and thought of the prayers of generations of Methodists that have been offered around the neat pulpit. Some I know were answered, like those that led to the final Act of Parliament in the 1830s to abolish slavery.

I felt at home there. Although I am now an Anglican, my mother's ancestors were Wesleyan Methodists from Swaledale in Yorkshire. The first chapel in Gunnerside was built in 1789, after John Wesley had made two visits, and the family name is one of the signatures on a petition sent to the House of Lords asking that slavery be abolished. In that part of Yorkshire, local people made their living from lead-mining, but others had emigrated to the new world of America and written home about the appalling cruelty of slavery that they saw there. I have seen a few of these letters from the emigrants, which always ended with the most fervent hope that although they would never meet again on earth, they might be 'reunited at the day of judgement'.

When we left the chapel a good hour later, the door was still open and people were still popping in. My friend Norman, their minister, was almost out on the street when he stopped and exclaimed, 'Oh dear, I haven't said my prayers yet,' and disappeared back into the 'quiet place' – to prepare for his day of judgement, too.

> *Gracious God,*
> *Whose glory is above all our thoughts*
> *and whose mercy is over all your works;*
> *May your Holy Spirit inspire our worship*
> *and make us attentive to your Word.*
> *Accept, we pray, the sacrifice of praise*
> *which your holy church offers to you this day.*
> *Being created by you,*
> *Let us ever act for your glory,*
> *and being redeemed by you,*
> *Let us render to you that which is your own;*
> *Through Jesus Christ our Lord. Amen*
> **from A Collection of Forms of Prayer (1733)**
> **by John Wesley**

I suspect that Cam Chapel is not on the 'must visit' list for tourists doing a lightning tour of Christian Britain. Neither is the ancient Collegiate Church of St Kentigern at Crichton, which stands near a ruined castle overlooking a wooded glen in Midlothian. Crichton Church is overshadowed by its more glamorous and – due to *The Da Vinci Code* – now world-famous sister chapel at Rosslyn, five miles away.

Like Rosslyn, Crichton was built – probably by Spanish stonemasons – to be a collegiate church, a church where a small community of lay priests would say Mass every day for the soul of its founder and benefactor. In Crichton's case, this was Sir William Crichton, Chancellor to King James II of Scotland, who established his college of priests in the church's lofty chancel in 1449. Unfortunately, Sir William was suspected of plotting against James IV in 1483 and lost all his estates, including the church and the handsome nearby castle.

Medieval Crichton continued as a church for the local parishioners, and shared its heyday with one of Scotland's greatest composers of church music, Robert Carver, but it is unlikely that prayers sung in Crichton ever achieved great musical heights.

> *O good Jesus, let not my sin destroy me.*
> *I beg you most holy Jesus,*
> *Forsake not me whom your love has made.*
> *O sweet Jesus, accept what is yours*
> *And reject that which offends you.*
> *O most beloved Jesus, O most longed for Jesus,*
> *O most gentle Jesus, O Jesus,*
> *Permit me to enter into your kingdom, sweet Jesus.*
>
> **from 'O bone Jesu'**
> **by Robert Carver (1485–1570)**

After the Scottish Reformation in 1560, the building at Crichton, by now in a state of considerable disrepair, was simply abandoned, and the congregation moved to a small stone room in a nearby wood. It was a practical solution to a practical problem. John Knox's *First Book of Discipline* centred everything on the Bible, 'the Word of God'. After the Reformation, the superintendents, who replaced bishops, ruled that 'we have thought it a thing most expedient' if, for example, the Kirk was in a ruinous state, that the congregation simply move to wherever there was room enough for the people to hear the preaching and the prayers. The word 'holy' now applied solely to the Bible, and no longer was a church thought of as a holy place: 'holiness' was experienced only whenever and wherever the Bible was open.

In the eighteenth and nineteenth centuries the church was brought back into use for worship, but the interior had to succumb to changing design schemes. False walls and galleries were put up and then taken down according to fashion, and the congregation was turned round to face in different directions, ending with its back to the original altar at the east end, to suit further 'things thought most expedient'.

This approach to worship almost sealed the fate of Crichton Collegiate Church again in 1992, when a crack opened up in the masonry of the church tower and the estimated cost to repair it was phenomenal. The then Church of Scotland minister declared the building unnecessary to his ministry, and the Kirk Session closed it. They already had a parish containing a historic ruin, another that had been overrun with dry rot, and two other churches.

For a time, Crichton Church lay closed and forlorn, much to the distress of many people from far and wide who had been baptized and married there, and also of those families whose forebears were commemorated on the war memorial or buried in the old churchyard. For them the idea of the church as the holy place still had great meaning.

Two years later, at a special service in the Kirk, the Church of Scotland officially handed the building over to the Crichton Collegiate Church Trust which, bringing together three Christian denominations, promised to make the building available to the whole community. The trust paid a symbolic £10 to the Church of Scotland, and took the building over in perpetuity. It was quite an alarming challenge; would the crack in the tower be a sign of more serious decay?

After more than ten years of hard work and prayer by a small group of people – which fortunately included a clever architect and a gifted musician – and a formidable amount of fund-raising, ranging from that church perennial, the coffee morning, to negotiations with charitable trusts, Historic Scotland and even the Lottery Fund, Crichton Collegiate Church is now fully restored. The Victorian stained glass from the 1890s restoration has been cleaned, and is once again the feature that attracts most visitors. Once again, the morning sun shines through the east window with its dramatic depiction of the agony in the Garden of Gethsemane.

BBC Radio 3 concerts and BBC Radio 4 *Sunday Worship* have been broadcast from the church. Animosity from the people who thought the building should remain closed has passed, and the present minister of the parish conducts at least one service each year at Crichton. He has even admitted that Crichton is the most beautiful church building in the area. It is, and is now recognized across Scotland as being among the nation's most historic kirks.

In 2005, a group of singers discovered another of Crichton Church's unique features: its acoustics. The huge stone-vaulted roof, which has survived local stone robbers and cannonballs and is as secure today as it was when it was built in 1445, now reflects the sound of prayers sung in the Taizé tradition. Each month a group of friends meets there to chant the rounds and choruses created by Brother Roger and his Taizé community in France. As they sing, they move around the church, breaking apart and listening to each other, creating beautiful harmonies. Then they stand – as do so many people who wander in on summer Sunday afternoons – in silence. In Crichton there are no formal tours or announcements. Lost in their own individual thoughts, all are offered the spiritual hospitality that the building has provided for more than 500 years.

> *Holy Spirit, you live in every human being*
> *And you come to place in us*
> *These essential realities of the Gospel:*
> *Kind-heartedness and forgiveness.*
>
> *To love and express it with our life,*
> *To love with kind heartedness and to forgive:*
> *There you will enable us to find*
> *One of the wellsprings of peace and joy.*
> **Brother Roger of Taizé (1915–2005)**

As Simone Weil wrote, 'To be rooted is perhaps the most important need of the human soul…'. In Upton Hellions, Cam Chapel and Crichton, as in thousands of other Christian places, our need for roots is met.

> *We love the place, O God,*
> *Wherein thine honour dwells;*
> *The joy of thine abode*
> *All earthly joy excels.*

from 'We love the place, O God' by William Bullock (1798–1874) and Henry Baker (1821–77)

Praying Together

· · · · · · · · · · · · ·

Completing the picture

Christ has no hands but our hands
To do his work today;
He has no feet but our feet
To lead all in his way.
Christ has no lips
To tell all how he died;
He has no help but our help
To bring them to his side
St Teresa of Avila

For any of the hundreds of thousands of people who have taken part in *Songs of Praise* over the last what will soon be half a century, St Teresa of Avila's prayer is very appropriate. It is only with the help of the hands, feet and lips of everyone assembled in range of the unblinking eye of the cameras that the programme is able to communicate their faith, hope and love to the millions who are watching.

Today it was not Christ's hands and feet that I was searching for, but his lips, because this evening temptation – in the form of a huge jigsaw puzzle – kept me from getting on with my writing. When all one thousand pieces are finally slotted into place, Liz and I are promised a magnificent view of the interior of St Paul's Cathedral. It was first of all the sound of 'God so loved the world' on *Songs of Praise* for Palm Sunday, coincidentally also coming from St Paul's, and perhaps the first ever contribution to the programme by the cathedral choir, that lured me downstairs, and then I could not resist trying to help Liz with her puzzle that depicts the east end. The edge pieces had all been found, and the statue of the apostle Paul was already visible, with his hand pointing upwards to the figure of God seated in glory, the centrepiece of the huge mosaic on the ceiling. But so far, all we had of God's face were his brow and two huge eyes staring sadly at us. Where were the pieces that would add the mouth and lips of the Creator? Having tried every piece spread out on the table, I realized that about 500 more pieces were lying completely unsorted in the box. There was clearly still a lot of work to be done. I went back upstairs to write about Christians praying together for the unity of churches, still divided after two thousand years of history.

Ever since the series began in 1961, *Songs of Praise* has made it a rule to invite singers from all the local churches to come together to take part. Often this has been hugely successful even, or rather especially, in Northern Ireland during the years when it was dominated by news of conflict. *Songs of Praise* was always able to show the hidden good news of Catholics and Protestants singing, praying and working together for peace and justice. But sometimes in unexpected places – in normally peaceful English villages – people still fall out during the weeks of preparation for *Songs of Praise*, as jealousies, disagreements and ancient animosities re-emerge. The puzzle still has to be completed before everyone is ready to sing together.

A hundred years ago, in fact just as jigsaw puzzles were becoming as popular and addictive in North America as Sudoko is today, a young Franciscan friar living in the USA felt that the time had come for Christians to give at least one week a year to praying for unity. By 1900 there were some early signs of common understanding between theologians, replacing centuries of conflict, but Paul Wattson knew that this new openness was not being experienced in the parishes. So while the jigsaw craze swept across the Western world – as children waited to see what new puzzle father had rented from the corner shop on his way home, and people even competed in clubs to complete the picture of the week – a Franciscan prayed for a solution to the greater puzzle of the divisions that had hampered the work and influence of the churches for so long.

The writer of John's Gospel describes how, after the Last Supper, Jesus prayed with his disciples. Yet, Jesus did not pray just for them:

'I ask not only on behalf of these, but also on behalf of those who will believe in me through their word, that they may all be one. As you, Father, are in me and I am in you, may they also be in us, so that the world may believe that you have sent me.'
John 17:20–21

When Paul Wattson and a nun, Mother Lurana White, formed the Franciscan Friars and Sisters of the Atonement, they felt in their study of this prayer that God was telling them that the journey to Christian unity would be a long and difficult one, and indeed at first they seemed to be getting nowhere. Then, in 1906, San Francisco was struck by the terrible earthquake and fire that shook the faith of many Christians. This seems to have been the catalyst that moved the American churches to begin wanting to pray together, and in January 1908 the first organized prayers for Christian unity were held. A hundred years later, always in the same week in January, from the feast of St Peter to the feast of St Paul, the Week of Prayer for Christian Unity is shared all around the world by Protestant, Orthodox and Roman Catholic churches.

Still inspired by the iconic image of Pope John Paul II and Archbishop Robert Runcie kneeling side by side in prayer at the altar in Canterbury Cathedral, in 1986 I helped the BBC's local radio stations to come together for six programmes in which all churches would try to listen to each other and pray for understanding and shared belief. The booklet that everyone would use included St Teresa of Avila's prayer, and there could have been no one better equipped to marshal an army of hands, feet and lips to turn her prayer into action than Canon Derek Palmer.

When I first met Derek, he was organizing Lent courses for BBC Radio Kent as well as being Archdeacon of Rochester. Derek, a larger than life personality in every respect, always arrived for the meetings with a bottomless supply of plans and ideas in his head, and he would put them across to us at breakneck speed, concluding with the words, 'Do y'see?'

We learnt quickly that whether or not we did see, we would still cheerfully be allocated a task and an alarmingly short space of time to do it in. Things began to happen; church doors began to open, if reluctantly at first. Why, after all, could not junior badminton in the church hall be cancelled for the first time in living memory, so that people from different churches could come together for a 'live' radio broadcast? Other senior church people – the theologian, Mary Tanner, and the late Martin Reardon, a saintly priest who more than anyone else managed to fulfil Derek's impossible deadlines – helped formulate the series of programmes of conversation and shared prayer.

The series title was to be 'What on earth is the church for?' I am sure it was Derek's idea, and that at first eyebrows were raised, but objections were all jovially waved aside. I had to carry Derek's message to persuade every BBC local radio station to join in, which involved a schedule of journeys that began to feel like Paul's. Every BBC station was competitive and proud of its distinctive individuality and, like the churches, they were far from sure that they wanted to come together at all. In the end, I think many of the station managers and the 230 volunteers, who joined together right across Britain, were won over by the intriguing title.

The plan was that everyone who took part (and in the end more than 1.3 million BBC listeners did) was to be asked an open-ended question: what, in the light of their experience, was the church doing to bring about the fulfilment of the prayer of Jesus recorded in John's Gospel, 'May they all be one…'?

It was one of the most extraordinary experiences of my life. People came together and shouted, wept and prayed with each other. People opened their homes to strangers from other churches and talked about the things that stopped them from worshipping together. Then they put them as questions to the speakers in the BBC studios. People told each other their own stories, sometimes for the first time, and many who took part all those years ago still meet to pray together.

As a result, the late Cardinal Hume led the English Roman Catholic Church, for the very first time, into membership of the ecumenical Council of Churches, with the Roman Catholic Church of Scotland and Wales joining too. His decision, announced in an impromptu contribution at a huge conference, came as a complete surprise to many. It was an answer to a prayer that had been used all through the six broadcasts by every group:

> *Lord God, we thank you*
> *For calling us into the company*
> *Of those who trust in Christ*
> *And seek to obey his will.*
> *May your spirit guide and strengthen us*
> *In mission and service to your world;*
> *For we are strangers no longer*
> *But pilgrims together*
> *On the way to your kingdom.*
> **Prayer for the National Lent Course of 1986**

In the third millennium, most people have perhaps forgotten the gale-force winds of the Spirit that Derek Palmer's prayers directed onto the British churches and the BBC's local radio network. Derek Palmer died suddenly in 2006, characteristically at an ecumenical gathering of churches in Oxfordshire, still using every ounce of energy to pursue the Christian unity that he so passionately believed in all his life.

Another great believer in the hope that one day all the churches could be one, and not just by being reunited with Rome, was the Franciscan Agnellus Andrew, a Roman Catholic bishop and one of the first to see the potential of religious broadcasting as a place of shared prayer. He used to say that most of the churches separated by disagreement had finally agreed to walk together through the foothills of their differences, but would now have to face up to mountainous difficulties that still lay ahead.

I remembered Bishop Andrew's warning recently, as I joined a small group of people from different churches for a two-day meeting to try to write a service for the centenary Week of Prayer for Christian Unity on the theme of 'pray without ceasing', taken from Paul's first letter to the Thessalonians. We began as strangers since we all come from widely differing backgrounds around Britain and Ireland. I was very apprehensive; I have always found the writing of prayers difficult, and the prospect of having to share my faltering thoughts with strangers was unappealing. I do not imagine Teresa of Avila wrote her prayers with a group of nuns contributing their thoughts. Some of the most flawed prayers and liturgies have emerged after different people have insisted on adding or subtracting words or, worst of all, when a new prayer has been put to the vote.

It soon became obvious in this group that it was the same for everyone else, as we all stared silently at our blank pieces of paper. Sometimes someone would suddenly say, to an already silent group, 'Just be quiet. I think I have an idea.' Thankfully, some were very good ideas.

One of the prayers that we all agreed should be in the first draft of the service was written by a much admired contributor to the work of Christian unity. Ian Fraser's prayer brings a discomforting insight into how far the churches still need to go. It was moving to be using his prayer in Scottish Churches House in Dunblane, a centre which he himself set up just yards from the cathedral where, in 1996, people from all persuasions prayed together in silence, after the tragic shooting of children in the town's primary school, that the world might be transformed.

Lord God,
Whose son was content to die
to bring new life,
have mercy on your church
which will do anything you ask,
anything at all,
except die
and be reborn.

Lord Christ,
forbid us unity
which leaves us where we are
and as we are:
welded into one company
but extracted from the battle;
engaged to be yours,
but not found at your side.

Holy Spirit of God,
reach deeper than our inertia and fears:
release us into the freedom of children of God.
Ian M. Fraser

In the first years of the new century, the news media has taken more and more interest in the churches, reporting division and crises within the different churches as well as between them. But even with tension between the Anglican churches of the West and those in the developing world, a prayer written in West Africa still expresses thanksgiving for neighbourliness throughout the world:

Lord, we thank you that our churches are like big families.
Lord, let your spirit of reconciliation blow over all the earth,

Let Christians live your love.
Lord, we praise you in Europe's cathedrals, in America's offering,
And in our African songs of praise.
Lord, we thank you that we have brothers and sisters in all the world.
Be with them that make peace. Amen
A prayer from West Africa

Stewart Cross was the only *Songs of Praise* television director who not only became a bishop, but also wrote hymns. The last verse of 'Father, Lord of all creation' is my prayer for every day of the Week of Prayer for Christian Unity, and for every *Songs of Praise* programme:

Holy Spirit, rushing, burning
Wind and flame of Pentecost,
Fire our hearts afresh with yearning
To regain what we have lost.
May your love unite our action,
Nevermore to speak alone:
God, in us abolish faction,
God, through us your love make known.
from 'Father, Lord of all creation' by Stewart Cross (1928–89)

Prayers at Sea

● ● ● ● ● ● ● ● ● ● ● ● ●

For those in peril

Dear God, be good to me;
The sea is so wide,
And my boat is so small.
Breton fisherman's prayer

This prayer always reminds me of a moment in *Songs of Praise* from the tiny harbour in the Cornish village of Coverack many years ago. As the cameras were set up for an afternoon of hymn singing, everyone was praying for good weather – no one more so than Liz, the director later to become my wife. She boarded a tiny boat with the film crew and an old fisherman, who was going to talk about his life and faith out at sea. The boat rapidly turned into a tiny dot as clouds began to appear and the wind rose. Liz tells me that they filmed tossing about for an hour in driving rain and wind, and when they had finished the interview and turned for home they realized that they had been sitting under the only cloud in the bay; just a few yards away the sun was shining and the sea was calm. They returned safely home, and in the edited programme viewers saw the old man in his little boat reappearing, bobbing across the waves as the choirs were singing 'Will your anchor hold?' Afterwards the fisherman described the experience as the most perfect of his life.

Anyone who sets sail from the safety of a small harbour into a huge sea needs to remember how swiftly the sea's mood can change. Down the centuries musicians have tried to express its dramatic power. Mendelssohn's overture 'A Calm Sea and a Prosperous Voyage' describes an idyllic journey with just enough breeze to fill the sails. You want to be there. From the first notes on the strings, a low reassuring murmur from the double basses, the listener can imagine azure waters stretching to a far horizon where past travellers without radar or sextant would hope to see a bank of cloud appear, indicating the presence of land and their destination. Trumpets herald a safe arrival: a wordless prayer of thanksgiving to God.

Yet when you listen to the wild and disturbed music that Benjamin Britten composed for 'The Storm', the last of the four sea interludes in his opera, *Peter Grimes*, the last thing you want is to be there, and it is reassuring to feel the heat of your own winter hearth. The composer was painting a picture in music of the treacherous, howling gales and tides that ate up the east coast of England where he lived and wrote so much of his music. The sea invaded his home more than once.

Here is a 500-year-old prayer for travellers by sea, and especially for those who, every hour of the day and night, have to venture out into deep waters:

> *O God, who didst bring our parents through the red sea*
> *And bear them through the great waters,*
> *We sing praise to thy name and humbly beseech thee*
> *That thou wouldst vouchsafe to turn away all adversities*
> *From thy servants travelling by sea, and to bring them unto the haven*
> *Where they would be.*
> **from The Sarum Missal**

Several hundred miles further up the east coast from Benjamin Britten's Norfolk, one morning last year several hundred people gathered on the harbour wall of the tiny fishing village of Cove, in eastern Scotland, to remember a great tragedy. People who live on this rocky, cliff-edged coast were marking the anniversary of a storm in which 199 men were lost at sea. From one port, Eyemouth, the sea took that night one in every three of the male population.

One hundred and twenty-five years later, the water was still and the North Sea gleamed in the sunlight. Taking her lead from the Gospel accounts of Jesus speaking to the crowd from a little boat, the minister leading the Service of Remembrance had gone to sea and moored a little way out, looking back at the congregation, who peered down from the harbour wall to see her in her little boat, as small as the one in which the Breton fishermen had prayed.

Peter Aitchison, a one-time colleague from BBC Scotland, was born in Eyemouth and in the course of researching his book about the disaster, *Children of the Sea*, has discovered that he was related to one of the fishermen who survived, a man known as Little Dod. He captures the atmosphere of the disaster with his first chapter heading: 'Sparkling Dawn, Damned Night'. The calm of Friday morning, 14 October 1881, did not fool the older fishermen in the town. They could sense a storm was brewing, but the fishing fleets still had to put out to sea: it was the town's livelihood.

The boats that were not overwhelmed and sunk in the first explosive minutes of the storm that night realized they would have to sail further out to sea, and keep well clear of the jagged rocks of the coastline. It became a desperate struggle for life. Aboard the *White Star*, Little Dod, the skipper, battled for hours to calm and organize his small, terrified crew. He was a local preacher, having been converted at a revival meeting, and all through the night he sang a hymn at the top of his voice. The words had become a desperate prayer for himself and his seven companions in the little boat:

> *Jesu, Lover of my soul,*
> *Let me to Thy bosom Fly,*
> *While the nearer waters roll,*
> *While the tempest still is high…*

They saw many of their friends' boats smashed to pieces. Men they knew drowned in front of their eyes. They could do nothing but pray. 'I knew that God held the great sea in the hollow of his hand and that he held the winds in his fist,' Little Dod wrote afterwards. Much later in the night, the wind suddenly dropped and the waters were stilled. At dawn, the *White Star* headed back to safety across a sea as innocent and beguiling as it was on the morning when I stood with the congregation at Cove Harbour and we sang the same hymn:

> *Hide me, O my saviour, hide,*
> *Till the storm of life is past,*
> *Safe into the haven guide;*
> *O receive my soul at last!*
> **from 'Jesu, Lover of my soul'**
> **by Charles Wesley (1707–88)**

A few days after the worst disaster that the east coast of Scotland had ever known, Little Dod, who became a respected community leader in Eyemouth, nodded to his crew to come aboard, and they set sail for the fishing ground again. A big fleet still regularly heads out from Eyemouth into a sea that is no less dangerous, but the community, which suffered so much on this 'Black Friday', will never be quite the same again.

> *Thou, O Lord, that stillest the raging of the sea,*
> *hear, hear us, and save us, that we perish not.*
> *O blessed Saviour, that didst save thy disciples ready to perish in a storm,*
> *hear us, and save us, we beseech thee.*
> **from *The Book of Common Prayer* (1662)**

This prayer was included in *The Book of Common Prayer* of the Church of England when it was revised in 1662. By then, there were so many British ships out at sea that there were not enough ministers to serve as chaplains, so this prayer was provided for the ship's captain to pray with the crew in times of danger.

———

From the dawn of civilization, people have feared the sea. Terrible monsters were once thought to be lurking in its depths. It was seen as the place of death, and the home of the devil. The story of the Israelites escaping from their Egyptian pursuers, when God parted the Red Sea to let them cross, had tremendous impact as a sign of the activity of the same creator who had flooded the whole earth, saving only Noah and the occupants of the ark. The disciples were in fear even of the inland Sea of Galilee and its storms.

As civilizations developed, people increasingly used the sea for travel. Christianity itself was largely spread across the world during the early centuries by men travelling by ship. Yet the sea always remained a place of mystery and danger. Daily reports in nineteenth-century newspapers reveal how dangerous a sea voyage could be. Before the invention of the sextant and the measurements of latitude and longitude, the moon was often the only clue for mariners to work out where they were. Some ships simply disappeared, or abandoned vessels would be seen floating by, like ghost-ships, and months later reports of these sightings would bring heart-breaking news:

The Mary Houghton, from Liverpool to Larne, has sunk off the coast of the Isle of Man; neither the master, his wife and family, who were on board, nor any of the crew have been heard of; her mast has been discovered above water, and on a diver being sent down her name was ascertained.

Pittenweem – Many small articles of bedding have drifted on shore in this neighbourhood, apparently foreign; also a Dutch Bible marked Pieter Fekker. Fishermen report having seen part of a vessel's stern at sea, and conjecture that a foreign vessel has been run down.

Sydney – The Waterwitch was wrecked on the Island of Uea, New Hebrides on January 20th; crew saved with the exception of some South Sea Islanders, whom the natives killed.
Shipping intelligence, published in ***The Daily Scotsman*** **(1857)**

One Sunday morning in 1982, on the far side of the Atlantic Ocean, the captain of a Royal Navy destroyer, HMS *Coventry*, led his crew in prayers.

> *O Eternal Lord God, who through many generations hast united and inspired the members of our Corps, grant thy blessing, we beseech thee, on Royal Marines serving all around the Globe. Bestow Thy Crown of Righteousness upon all our efforts and endeavours, and may our Laurels be those of gallantry and honour, loyalty and courage. We ask these things in the name of Him, whose courage never failed, our Redeemer, Jesus Christ. Amen.*
The prayer of Her Majesty's Royal Marines

Very soon afterwards, HMS *Coventry* came under a devastating attack. Nineteen members of the ship's company died when, after only fifteen minutes of the onslaught, the ship sank. Miraculously, though, the majority were saved.

Since *Songs of Praise* began, it has regularly made programmes about the lives of Britain's seafarers, lifeboat men, fishermen and the Royal Navy. Some of the most perilous times for those at sea were during the battles of the Falklands War. Many ships were hit, and three weeks before the end, bombers destroyed the support ship, *Sir Galahad*, and the destroyer, HMS *Coventry*, on which prayers had been shared by the ship's company. The Cross of Nails, given to the ship's company by Coventry Cathedral and displayed in pride of place, was lost. Today, those who died are remembered on nearby Pebble Island, where a huge cross resembling the nails of the bombed cathedral's roof is a place of pilgrimage and prayer for veterans of the campaign.

The flagship of the Task Force was the huge carrier, HMS *Hermes*, one of the oldest and largest ships and almost a sitting target; on three occasions the Argentinean forces claimed to have sunk her. Roger Devonshire, now retired, travelled out from Portsmouth on 5 April 1982, along with many highly trained but anxious men wondering what they would have to face. He was one of two chaplains who had the spiritual care of the 1,500 men on *Hermes*.

Once they arrived in the waters of the exclusion zone around the islands then occupied by the Argentinean forces, they were frequently in imminent danger. At least twice a day the alarm would sound, indicating the presence of missile-launching aircraft, and the whole crew would have to go to 'action stations'. The captain of HMS *Hermes* had placed the ship's chapel out of bounds – it was below the waterline, and if the ship was bombed, everyone in the chapel would have been trapped – so Roger Devonshire organized his daily communion services in his own small cabin.

Each service began with people jammed in so tightly that the chaplain could scarcely move his hands at the improvised altar, a chest of drawers. One evening, just at the end of the Prayer of Confession, the klaxon sounded 'action stations', its deafening rasp destroying the silence that had followed the prayer.

Most merciful God,
Father of our Lord Jesus Christ,
we confess that we have sinned
in thought, word and deed.
We have not loved you with our whole heart.
We have not loved our neighbours as ourselves.
In your mercy
forgive what we have been,
help us to amend what we are,
and direct what we shall be;

that we may do justly,
love mercy,
and walk humbly with you, our God.
Amen.
Prayer of Confession, from *Common Worship* (2000)

The cabin emptied in a flash as everyone rushed to defend the huge ship against her attackers. Two and a half hours later, HMS *Hermes* was still afloat and yet another panic was over. When the chaplain returned to his cabin, he could not get near it. Everyone had come back to hear the prayer of absolution.

Even on brief visits to warships, I have been struck by the noise and the claustrophobia. Once, on an aircraft carrier very like *Hermes*, I stood on the huge lift that took aircraft down to the hangar in the hull. It was like descending into hell, the fresh air replaced by heat, oil fumes and noise. On a ship at 'action stations', there is nowhere to go and nothing to do except prepare to do your part. Every second must have seemed like a lifetime. But they made time for the prayer and reflection that we, in safety, never seem to find time for:

God, beyond our dreams, you have stirred in us a mem'ry,
You have placed your powerful spirit in the hearts of humankind.
All around us we have known you;
All creation lives to hold you.
In our living and our dying
We are bringing you to birth.
from 'God beyond all names' by Bernadette Farrell (b. 1957)

Back in Britain in 1982, before the instant global information transmissions that viewers nowadays expect, news travelled slowly back from the Falklands. At regular intervals on BBC One, announcements from the Ministry of Defence were read out in carefully neutral, measured tones by Ian Macdonald. His appearances were often unexpected, and one Sunday morning he suddenly interrupted prayers on the live Sunday morning worship programme, *This is the Day*. His grim intervention heralding further casualties created the most fervent wave of shared prayer that the programme had ever known.

The end of that mercifully short but terrible conflict in 1982 was marked by *Songs of Praise* coming from the South Atlantic, with the final hymn – 'Eternal Father strong to save' (What else?) – sung on the open deck of one of the Royal Navy ships that had helped liberate the islands. At last, it was safe to stand in the open air on the San Carlos Water and sing hymns of thanksgiving, where for weeks anxious watch had been maintained night and day. The prayer expressed in the final verse of 'Eternal Father', with its tune 'Melita' recalling Paul's shipwreck on the coast of Malta, has a particular place in the heart of every sailor:

O Trinity of love and power,
Our brethren shield in danger's hour;
From rock and tempest, fire and foe,
Protect them wheresoe'er they go:
And ever let there rise to thee
Glad hymns of praise from land and sea.
from 'Eternal Father strong to save' by William Whiting (1825–78)

Hymns

• • • • • • • • • • • • •

Songs of praise

A good hymn should be like a good prayer – simple, real, earnest and reverent.
Bishop Walsham How (1823–97)

Amazing grace! How sweet the sound
That saved a wretch like me;
I once was lost, but now am found,
Was blind, but now I see.
John Newton (1725–1807)

It was no surprise when 'Amazing Grace' was voted in the top forty of the 'Nation's Favourite Hymns'. It tells a story that is both extraordinary and yet somehow familiar to everyone, and many *Songs of Praise* viewers have told me that they use the hymn as a prayer. Each verse describes a life that has fallen short of what the inner small voice of conscience demands, but by the grace of God, everything has changed, sins are forgiven, and a new life is promised. Finally, there is the hint of heaven:

The earth shall soon dissolve like snow,
the sun forbear to shine,
but God who called me here below,
will be for ever mine.

If you know this hymn as it appears in the hymnal, you will realize that I have ended the hymn at verse five. That is because this was the end of John Newton's own verses. The sixth verse, however spiritually uplifting, originally belongs to a completely different hymn.

'Amazing Grace' is the autobiography of a man who grew up in the dangerous world of eighteenth-century seafaring, was press-ganged onto a Royal Navy ship and later became captain of an African slave ship. The story of how this violent man – who entertained seaman with his songs lampooning their superiors – came to write a hymn was described by the musician Rick Wakeman in a Holy Week programme on BBC One.

Newton's own faith, and the hymn itself, began during a terrible storm at sea, as he and the crew fought to save the ship from being overwhelmed. 'If this will not do,' Newton told the captain, 'then the Lord have mercy on us.' At that moment Newton wrote, 'I knew that there was a God.'

> 'Twas grace that taught my heart to fear;
> and grace my fears relieved;
> how precious did that grace appear;
> the hour I first believed!

The ship and her crew survived, but it was to be another twenty-five years before Newton wrote the hymn with the verse describing 'the hour' he had experienced on that voyage. Although he now believed in God, Newton still went on trading slaves. It was several years later that his reading of the Bible made him realize that he was still a 'wretch', still a 'bondsman', because although he might now do it in more considerate ways, he relied for his existence on slave-trading.

By 1773, John Newton had renounced his past, been ordained and would soon meet William Wilberforce, whose campaign to abolish the slave trade had already begun. On 1 January 1773, as Revd John Newton, he preached a sermon to his congregation in the Buckinghamshire village of Olney, on the theme of 'past mercies and future hopes'.

Through many dangers, toils and snares
I have already come:
'tis grace that brought me safe thus far,
and grace will lead me home.

His sermon became the basis for the hymn, which is now one of the most popular songs in the world. But the words that Newton taught line by line to his choir were certainly not sung to the tune we are familiar with today. The hymn was published in New York in the 1780s, but then disappeared from general use for almost 200 years until 1971, when the singer Judy Collins found it and sang it in church one day, and a recording was made.

When we've been there a thousand years,
Bright shining as the sun,
we've no less days to sing God's praise
than when we first begun.

Where does this extra verse come from? It first appeared in 1850, in Harriet Beecher Stowe's famous anti-slavery novel, *Uncle Tom's Cabin*, but it was not much sung. Rick Wakeman thinks that it originally comes from 'Jerusalem, my happy home', a hymn that is rarely sung these days because it has twenty-six verses! Based on the book of Revelation, it was translated from an ancient Latin poem in the sixteenth century by a Roman Catholic priest, known only by his initials, F.B.P. He goes to enormous lengths to describe a rather wistful vision of heaven, which the writer seems much less sure of attaining than the seaman who had experienced sudden saving grace in a storm at sea. It can certainly be sung to the same tune, but the verse above is not included in any of the versions that I have seen.

The clue to the mystery is found in a reference in an American book to a Revd Joseph Bromehead, who in 1795 'added joys of his own', that is to say, yet more verses to 'Jerusalem, my happy home'. Clearly it was a habit of this unknown clergyman to add verses to other people's hymns, and he was inspired to add 'joys of his own' to 'Amazing Grace', so that this hymn, rooted in a deeply personal experience, concludes with the verse that is a universal prayer.

———

There is another hymn whose tune, much better known than the words, has itself become a wordless prayer – this time from the twentieth century. The tune's fame stems from its link with a tragic event. At 2 a.m. on a September morning in 1934, a wall of fire swept through Gresford Pit in North Wales, killing 266 miners in one of the worst-ever colliery disasters. Two years later, a fellow miner from the north-east of England composed a tune for his local brass band and named it 'Gresford', dedicating it to the memory of those who had died in the disaster.

> O Saviour Christ, who on the cruel tree
> For all mankind thy precious blood has shed,
> In Life Eternal trusting, we
> To thy safe keeping leave our dead.

Since then, various sets of words, including the ones above, have been sung to his composition, but it takes no more than the playing of the tune to create an atmosphere of reflection and prayer. For anyone whose life and work has revolved around the dangers and comradeship of mining coal far underground, it has become as significant as the two-minute silence of Remembrance Sunday.

Every year on a Saturday in July, Durham's cricket ground is transformed when thousands of former miners and working people from other industries march onto the ground for the Miners' Gala. Once there were a hundred pits in County Durham. Now all have closed – but this has not stopped the gala. In past years up to 250,000 people would invade Durham on gala day for 'The Big Meeting', increasing the population of the city six-fold.

Even in the changed world of 2006, 50,000 people were milling about the city when I was there in July. Thirty or more brass bands, many made up of ex-miners, marched through the streets escorting fifty huge and colourful hand-made banners. There are two sides to every banner: one depicts the famous trade unionists and politicians who fought for the miners, and on the other there are symbols of Christian faith, sometimes scenes from the Bible and sometimes the reassuring solidity of Durham's great cathedral of St Cuthbert.

This building, visible for miles around, may have done something to penetrate and warm 'the frosted foreboding of men on the early morning shift' before they descended into the darkness. For many of the old miners, their hard lives were sustained by prayer as much as by brotherly solidarity, and the church and working people still walk together in the north-east of England.

On the cricket ground in July, politicians and trade unionists had assembled on a platform; but before they displayed their powers of oratory with more than an echo of the old revivalist preachers, the Lord Mayor of Durham arrived. Everyone fell silent at the gala president's opening words: 'Comrades, we stand for Gresford.'

As the band struck up, everyone on the cricket ground stood still; it is an honour to be chosen to play. As the musicians played six different versions of the tune, including a moving cornet solo, the huge crowd quietly remembered all the miners whose lives were lost in the pits.

Later, while the rally was still hearing a message for the Palestinian people, I noticed four of the bands, with some of the most beautiful banners, form up and steal away. Once in the street outside, I learnt that their sights were set on the cathedral high above the city. Each banner, newly made to commemorate the continuing life of former mining communities, was to be taken to the mother church of the diocese, where the Bishop of Durham would bless them.

Outside the cathedral, half an hour before the service started, there was an ominous sign that read, 'Queue here for the Gala Service'. After more than a century, the Gala Service has become a red-letter day in the cathedral's year. Once we had all been squeezed in, we sat in silence until, with a drumbeat, an extraordinary procession started. A brass band came first, the musicians as smart and impressive as the Brigade of Guards, moving up the huge Norman nave at a slow march towards the waiting bishop. Behind them was a new banner held up by four standard-bearers. The banner was huge and clearly difficult to keep under control. Helping to hold it up were three generations of proud men – grandfathers, veterans of the pits, with their children and grandchildren.

It was once again a hymn tune that brought the tears to many eyes, including mine. The tune 'Alberta' is sung to Cardinal Newman's great hymn 'Lead kindly light', but we did not need to sing the words to feel a bond with these communities that have survived so many years of hardship, with the fathers and grandfathers who for so many generations worked down in the dark, guided only by a miner's lamp.

> *Lead kindly light, amid the encircling gloom,*
> *Lead thou me on;*
> *The night is dark, and I am far from home,*
> *Lead thou me on.*
> *Keep thou my feet; I do not ask to see*
> *The distant scene; one step enough for me.*
> **from 'Lead kindly light' by John Henry Newman (1801–90)**

Bernadette Farrell is one of the best-known hymn writers of our time. She was interviewed on *Songs of Praise* in a programme in which Pam Rhodes looked at the work and inspiration of women hymn writers. I first encountered her music one morning while listening on my car radio to BBC Radio 4's *Daily Service*. On the long-wave frequency, this can often be like hearing a programme in a severe hailstorm, but the reception sometimes improves. This it did, and as I slowly inched towards a busy roundabout, getting close to the front of the queue, the following words were sung:

Longing for light, we wait in darkness.
Longing for truth, we turn to you.
Make us your own people,
Light for the world to see.

Christ, be our light!
Shine in our hearts.
Shine through the darkness.
Christ, be our light!
Shine in your Church gathered today.
from 'Christ, be our light' by Bernadette Farrell (b. 1957)

'I always write for the moment,' says Bernadette, although probably not meaning the moment when a motorist escapes from a busy roundabout. Hearing it that day supercharged my energies at the beginning of a long journey. The chorus is easy to remember, and stayed with me all the way on my 100-mile journey from Edinburgh to Carlisle.

I now know why the words of 'Christ, be our light' are so easy to learn: the hymn was written for a congregation who, to begin with, would be in almost total darkness. The new Roman Catholic church of St Gabriel in Upper Holloway, North London, was being consecrated, and they would be singing this new hymn by the light of the paschal candle, the big candle first lit at dawn on Easter Day. As the hymn was sung, candles positioned all around the walls of the new church would be lit, so that the congregation would be introduced to their new home. Finally, the light of the paschal candle would light little candles held by the congregation. They, as Bernadette had intended, were the 'light of the world'.

With very little rehearsal everyone soon knew the chorus and was able to use their eyes not to read the words, but to watch the light spread. It must have been moving and spectacular.

Longing for shelter, many are homeless.
Longing for warmth, many are cold.
Make us your building, sheltering others,
Walls made of living stone.
Bernadette Farrell (b. 1957)

Since then, 'Christ, be our light' has been translated into many languages, including Chinese and Vietnamese. However, the response to the first time it was sung gives its writer the greatest satisfaction. After that service, people from St Gabriel's and their visitors from neighbouring churches began to discuss how they could help the many homeless in the area. They had their new building, and they knew that many people who would come for an hour on Sunday to worship there had no homes to go back to. They could come into the warm for a smile and a chat, but that night the congregation thought of a way that they could really help them in their new church. Above all, people living in hostels, bed-sits, or out on the streets need a place to wash, shower and find clean clothes. So now, built into the roof of the church hall, are six showers each for men and women.

It was like an answer to prayer, and although Bernadette claims no credit, she secretly hopes that her hymn may have been part of it.

Bless, O God,
those who with hymns and psalms and spiritual songs
make melody in their hearts to you.
May their anthems of praise be one
with the songs of the saints in light;
through Jesus Christ our Lord. Amen.
Norman Wallwork

Prayer and the Saints

· · · · · · · · · · · · ·

Virtuous and godly living

Almighty God,
who hast knit together thine elect in one communion and fellowship,
in the mystical body of thy Son, Christ our Lord:
grant us grace so to follow
thy blessed Saints in all virtuous and godly living,
that we may come to those unspeakable joys,
which thou hast prepared
for them that unfeignedly love thee;
through Jesus Christ our Lord.
Collect for All Saints Day, from *The Book of Common Prayer* (1662)

One of the stranger experiences of working on church committees is when you all sit around a boardroom table trying to make a list of saints. This happens whenever a denomination, or in my own case, *all* the denominations in Scotland, have decided to prepare a list of Sundays on which particular people will be remembered. Around the table, everyone racks their brains. Rather irreverently, it reminds me of BBC radio's *Desert Island Discs*: which eight noble and holy men and women should we include? The list of people who we each think have brought God into the life of the church quickly grows.

Many men and women whom the churches remember on a particular day each year have been martyred for their faith. Janani Luwum, remembered by the Anglican Church on 17 February, was a teacher. He was ordained in 1956, and by 1974 had become Archbishop of Uganda, at that time a country in the hands of Idi Amin. Three years later the archbishop, who had become one of the dictator's sternest critics as thousands of innocent people were being murdered, was killed in a car crash engineered by Idi Amin.

ARCHBISHOP LUWUM 1922–1977

God of truth,
Whose servant Janani Luwum walked in the light,
And in his death defied the powers of darkness:
Free us from fear of those who kill the body,
That we too may walk as children of light,
Through him who overcame darkness
By the power of the cross,
Jesus Christ your Son our Lord,
Who is alive and reigns with you,
In the unity of the Holy Spirit,
One God, now and for ever.
from *Exciting Holiness* (1997)

Thomas Cranmer, who was to become Archbishop of Canterbury in 1533, and became a strong supporter of the Reformation, was the compiler of two versions of the Church of England *Book of Common Prayer*, in 1549 and in 1552. It is to him that we owe the poetic language of so many prayers that are included in this book and are still in daily use all over the world. Having supported Henry VIII at the time when the Catholic Church in England broke away from Rome, he was convicted of treason and heresy in the reign of the Roman Catholic Queen Mary. Having first recanted his Protestant faith, he then withdrew his confession, and died embracing the Reformation.

THOMAS CRANMER 1489–1556

Father of all mercies,
Who through the work of your servant Thomas Cranmer
Renewed the worship of your Church
And through his death revealed your strength in human weakness:
By your grace strengthen us to worship you
In spirit and in truth
And so to come to the joys of your everlasting kingdom;
Through Jesus Christ our Mediator and Advocate,
Who is alive and reigns with you,
In the unity of the Holy Spirit,
One God, now and for ever.

**Collect marking the death at the stake of Thomas Cranmer
on 21 March 1556, from** *Exciting Holiness* **(1997)**

St Swithun was a learned monk who became Bishop of Winchester at the beginning of the ninth century. He was a humble man, who should perhaps be remembered for his great learning and the piety of his life, but is in fact probably only remembered on 15 July each year – in the weather forecast. If it rains on St Swithun's Day, so the saying goes, it will rain for the following forty days. His reputation as a 'weather saint' was created when Ethelwold, a later Bishop of Winchester, wanted to remove St Swithun's bones from the churchyard of the Old Minster – where he had been buried at his own desire, and where 'passers by might tread and where the rain from the eaves might fall on it' – to a golden shrine in the fine new cathedral that had just been built. In spite of warnings of violent storms if he moved the saint, Ethelwold went ahead, but the whole process was much delayed by almost incessant rain.

ST SWITHUN died 2 July AD 862

Almighty God,
by whose grace we celebrate again

the feast of our servant Swithun:
grant that, as he governed with gentleness
the people committed to his care,
so we, rejoicing in our Christian inheritance,
may always seek to build up your Church in unity and love;
through Jesus Christ your Son our Lord,
who is alive and reigns with you,
in the unity of the Holy Spirit,
one God, now and for ever.
from *Exciting Holiness* (1997)

Hilda, known in her own time as Hild, was born in AD 614 into the royal surroundings of the kingdom of Northumbria. She was baptized in York by Paulinus, who founded the minster. At the age of thirty-three she became a nun and set up an unusual abbey in Whitby, to house both monks and nuns. It was an important centre of learning, but what we most owe to Hilda today is that in AD 664 she called together the Synod of Whitby. Working through all sorts of technical information about the phases of the moon, they eventually came up with the formula to settle when Easter should be observed. The agreement they forged then is still in place, except in the Orthodox churches, which have gone their own way.

Hilda's commitment to getting the date settled was said to have been inspired by a husband and wife who had fallen out because one partner was still in Lent while the other was celebrating Easter. She is remembered on 19 November every year.

HILDA OF WHITBY AD 614–80
Eternal God,
Who made the abbess Hilda to shine like a jewel
And through her holiness and leadership
Blessed your Church with new life and unity:
Help us, like her, to yearn for the gospel of Christ

And to reconcile those who are divided;
Through him who is alive and reigns with you,
In the unity of the Holy Spirit,
One God, now and for ever.
from *Exciting Holiness* (1997)

Saints are often assumed to be outside our own time – heroic figures of the past whose deeds and lifestyles seem to be far beyond our own capabilities. Some people not described officially as saints but remembered in prayer by the churches, such as the eighteenth-century MP William Wilberforce, have, by their faith, had a huge impact on the current world. Wilberforce's commitment to fighting the evils of slavery is expressed in one of his own family prayers:

> *Almighty God, may we live above the world, its low concerns and unsatisfying vanities, and may we be still endeavouring to please thee, to root out every remainder of our natural corruption, and to increase in every Christian grace. May we indeed bear about us the likeness of our heavenly Father, and be doing good according to the will of God, until at length thou shalt receive us to thyself, and make us partakers of those pleasures which are at thy right hand for evermore.*
> **William Wilberforce**

Other people whom I would call saints may now be quite unknown. I have a few yellowed pages of a diary written by a church caretaker in an air raid shelter in 1941. The writer, referred to as 'L', describes the terrible bombing of Manchester, which began as the congregation of Lawton Moor Methodist Church gathered to sing Christmas carols on Sunday evening, 22 December 1940. As the choir sang 'Silent Night', gunfire was heard. The preacher announced the text for his sermon, but said anyone who was frightened should leave. No one moved. 'We looked at each other, smiled and sat still,' 'L' writes.

Apparently, by the end of the service the bombing had become so bad that everyone was trapped. 'L' records that he 'conducted community hymn singing until 10.30 p.m.'. By then, the congregation had been 'magically' fed, and the church reorganized so that everyone could sleep in some sort of safety. Children lay tucked up in carpets on cushions taken from the communion rail in the vestry, and the preacher slept near a radiator. 'Spasmodic snoring was heard until 6.30 a.m. when the "all-clear" sounded.'

Amazingly, everyone got up and prepared to go to work. The city was devastated. People walked through the wrecked streets calling out to each other. 'L' called out to a neighbour, 'How have you got on?' The neighbour replied, 'Oh, we are still alive, but we have no home.' The conductor of one of the few buses said, 'Some of you folks are paying fares for nothing to places in town last night, not there this morning!'

I know nothing else about 'L'. There were more raids to come and he may not have survived. As he sheltered from the bombs, he ended his account: 'Business is "as usual" and we pray for real "silent nights – holy nights" when we can consider the moon and the stars, God's handiwork, without any fears of the terrors of the night.' I think that there were saints in Manchester that Christmas – or at the very least, candidates for the *Songs of Praise* series 'Unsung Heroes'.

Some churches do not accept the idea of saints at all. For them, Jesus is the only mediator between God and us, and prayers to the saints or the Virgin Mary are simply unacceptable. Having met Mother Teresa of Calcutta – who may, in the future, be declared a saint by the Roman Catholic Church – I can only say that for me she was more than just an extraordinarily good person. Her simple lifestyle and her care for the poor and the dying, against all odds and at the expense of everything else in life, are well known, but she embodied something more. 'I want to help. But how do you start?' I asked her. She completely stopped me in my tracks when she replied, 'You start with the one next to you.'

O when the saints go marching in,
O when the saints go marching in;
O Lord, I want to be in that number
When the saints go marching in!

Traditional

Prayer in War

• • • • • • • • • • • • •

Valiant hearts

'Call to remembrance, O Lord, thy tender mercies:
and thy lovingkindnesses, which have been of old.
Let not our enemies triumph over us.
Deliver us, O Lord God of Israel, out of all our troubles.'
'In Time of War', from Psalm 25:6, 2, 22,
***Sarum Missal* in English (c. 1300)**

This is one of the first English language prayers that congregations heard
their priest say in the days when war swept backwards and forwards across
Britain. Enemy armies would appear unannounced, burning and
destroying towns and villages, so every churchgoer would listen to these
verses from the Psalms, hoping fervently for their own safety.

Two hundred years later, in 1513, King Henry VIII wrote his own
prayer for victory as he led his army to invade France. He took with him
the whole choir of the Chapel Royal, whose boys still join the Queen and
her family at the Cenotaph on Remembrance Sunday.

Pray we to God that all may gyde
That for our kyng so to provide
To send hym power to hys corage
He may acheffe this gret viage:

Now let us syng this rownd all thre;
Sent George, graunt hym the victory.
King Henry VIII

Four centuries ago, in June 1544, Archbishop Thomas Cranmer issued the first official version of 'The Litany in English'. Henry VIII had been displeased that his people were slack in their prayers for him and for relief from the wars and pestilences of the time. Their excuse was that the litany was in Latin and not understood, so 'Certain Godly Prayers' were to be recited as the congregation walked in procession, and all responded 'Good Lord, deliver us' after each prayer.

From battayle and from sudden death:
Good Lord, deliver us.
Thomas Cranmer, *Litany of Prayer* **(1544)**

The traditional-language *Book of Common Prayer* of the Church of England, which was ordered to be used in every English church three times a week, still contains almost word for word Cranmer's original translation from the Latin. It is still used in some churches twice a year. As the season of Advent began in 2006, the congregation of St Mary's Cathedral in Edinburgh prayed with the choir, 'Good Lord, deliver us', while Norman Wickham, an eighty-one-year-old priest – frail in body but with a wonderful singing voice – walked slowly through the nave proclaiming our 'Godly Prayers'. For the cathedral, the litany will never be the same again, because Norman, who served in the Royal Navy in the Second World War, died soon afterwards. Today, the members of St Mary's may not feel the great personal impact of the petition against battle and sudden death that people would have felt in the sixteenth century. After the nearby Battle of Pinkie in 1549, for instance, thousands in both armies died as the English defeated the Scots, having tried to get them to agree to a union between the two nations. War at home was in those days a constant and terrifying likelihood.

As time went by, the litany processions became increasingly disorganized and disorderly, and congregations were ordered to kneel instead. Then the English prayers and the English language services themselves became the subject of rebellion, especially in Cornwall, where congregations took up arms rather than lose their old Latin church services. It was a battle that they lost, one of many in the great, long-running war between Protestants and Catholics, in which the words and gestures of worship would sometimes bring about the downfall of kings and queens.

More than a century after Cranmer's first translations were made, after decades of civil war in Britain, the Restoration of the monarchy brought in a brief period of peace, order and harmony for public prayer:

> *O most powerful and glorious Lord God, the Lord of hosts, that rulest and commandest all things; Thou sittest in the throne judging right, and therefore we make our address to Thy Divine Majesty in this our necessity, that Thou wouldest take the cause into Thine own hands, and judge between us and our enemies. Stir up Thy strength, O Lord, and come and help us; for Thou givest not always the battle to the strong, but canst save by many or by few.*
>
> *O let not our sins now cry against us for vengeance; but hear us, Thy poor servants, begging mercy and imploring Thy help, and that Thou wouldst be a defence unto us against the face of the enemy.*
>
> *Make it appear that Thou art our Saviour and mighty Deliverer,*
> *Through Jesus Christ our Lord. Amen*
> from **The Book of Common Prayer** (1662)

This new prayer, to be said in times of conflict, appeared when *The Book of Common Prayer* was revised and re-introduced in the Church of England at the Restoration. It replaced what was called 'the puritan wail', shouted by soldiers of Oliver Cromwell's army before the start of the many cruel and violent battles across the countryside in which about one-third of the male population had perished. Might was no longer right, even when the cause was just.

Today, at least for Remembrance Sunday, we try to make our prayers less chauvinistic than in earlier centuries. As we remember all who have died in war and terrorism, we also pray for peace and justice for all the nations of the world, and ask God to help us pray for those 'who wish us harm':

> *O God of truth and justice,*
> *we hold before you those whose memory*
> *we cherish,*
> *and those whose names we will never know.*
> *Help us to lift our eyes above the torment*
> *of this broken world,*
> *and grant us the grace to pray for those*
> *who wish us harm.*
> *As we honour the past, may we put our*
> *faith in your future;*
> *for you are the source of life and hope,*
> *now and for ever.*
> **From an order of service (2005) for the churches of Britain and Ireland for Remembrance Sunday**

———

In 1939, for the second time in a century, the whole world was at war.

Father forgive them, for they know not what they do.
Luke 23:34, used as a prayer in a Japanese internment camp

The words of Christ on the cross were spoken as a prayer by a young curate, small in stature and in poor health, in Holy Week 1945. He, along with thousands of other inhabitants of Singapore, had been in Japanese hands since February 1942.

On 10 October 1943, Japanese guards came in the middle of the night to arrest many people. They were convinced that a secret radio transmitter was being operated by the prisoners and was sending intelligence to the Allies. One of those arrested was the Anglican Bishop of Singapore, Leonard Wilson, to whom John Hayter was chaplain. Bishop Wilson disappeared for several months while he was being interrogated. 'Why does your God not save you?' his torturers screamed. He replied, 'He does save me, but not from pain. He saves me by giving me the spirit to bear it.'

There *was* a radio hidden in the camp, but it was only capable of receiving the BBC World Service. The man who had built the receiver gave himself up, and was executed.

Almost three years after his capture, on his thirtieth birthday, John Hayter, living in prison hut 131 with a hundred other men, had become emaciated. Medicine was almost non-existent and food supplies had begun to run out. The Camp Commandant, General Saito, had warned them that they would now have to fend for themselves. The meagre rice ration was cut by 20 per cent in February 1945. A month later another cut coincided with the news that some women, wives of men in the camp, had died in another prison.

As John Hayter preached to a large crowd in the Holy Week service held in the open air at Sime Road Camp, the air was filled with rumours. The Allies had been seen bombing the nearby city for several months, and yet they were all still trapped. There were 4,000 men, women and children held in captivity, and another 1,000 prisoners had arrived during that Lent; rumours were circulating of further planned marches into the jungle, into which so many prisoners of war had already been marched, and from where, so far, they had never returned. In perilous circumstances out of their control, and with no hope that they would ever be free, their prayers took a quite different form from that of the church in the mid-seventeenth century. John Hayter wrote in the tiny diary that he managed to hide from his captors, 'We hate and never can forget so many of the evils committed by the Japanese, but hatred is a bad bed-fellow for any Christian.'

In the notes for his sermon, preached to hundreds of fellow prisoners in the camp yard that uneasy and strange Holy Week, he spoke about forgiveness:

We are slow to understand that forgiveness carries with it far more than an attitude of genial and irresponsible magnanimity. Not a 'forgive and forget' attitude, but an attitude and a course of action which wishes the best for others, even in the face of repeated wrong being done. And there are some things we find practically impossible to forgive. We here in the Camp mourn the death of some of our number at the hands of the Kampei-Tai and there are still some under arrest about whom we are desperately anxious. Others, thank God, have returned to us, but bearing in their bodies the marks of their suffering.

John Hayter and Bishop Wilson both survived, and for the rest of their lives never spoke of their imprisonment without mentioning how it would have been much worse had not a Japanese Christian, Lieutenant Andrew Ogawa, frequently risked his own life to help them. It was he who had ensured that worship was permitted, and several men escaped death at the hands of the secret police because of him.

John Hayter was to become very ill in the last months of his internment, but recovered to return home, and for twenty-seven years was a much-loved vicar of Boldre in the New Forest. When he appeared on BBC One on *This is the Day*, and again in an interview with Sir Harry Secombe not long before he died, his thoughts were the same as those he had used to finish the sermon in Holy Week 1945, when he was still in enemy hands:

One thing is clear from that lonely cross on a hill-top, the symbol of all that is best: the gravity of the wrong done can never be a barrier to forgiveness. Every time we use the words 'Our Father', we hear Christ's 'Love your enemies, bless them that curse you, do good to them that hate you and pray for them that despitefully use you and persecute you.'

Bring them to a right mind, O Father.
Help them to know what is involved in peaceful living.
Grant them that they may know you and play their part in
building a better world. Amen.

After the war, John Hayter and Bishop Wilson baptized some of their former captors who had become converts to Christianity.

O God, our help in ages past,
Our hope for years to come,
Be thou our guard while troubles last,
and our eternal home.
from 'O God, our help in ages past' by Isaac Watts (1674–1748)

Praying Alone

● ● ● ● ● ● ● ● ● ● ● ● ● ●

Prayers of the heart

Holy God,
Holy strong,
Holy immortal,
Have mercy on us.
The *Trisagion*, from the Orthodox Church

Patricia Frank sits surrounded by photographs of the people she loves and prays for. They cover a whole wall. When she wakes up in the morning, the first things her eyes light on are photographs of John, her late husband, and Pat, her late father. Both were priests in the Anglican Church, her father better known as Pat McCormick, a greatly loved religious broadcaster from the 1920s and 1930s. A friendly face looks down at us from the wall in the sitting room as we talk about her memories of him.

My eye is distracted by the view of a beautiful lake outside her window. Once one of London's docks, it is now home to swans and seagulls, and glitters in the sun. I cannot imagine getting much work done in a room with such a view, but Patricia, even in her nineties, is still working away here every day, and has recently completed two long poems. Nick Holtam, the present rector of St Martin-in-the-Fields, where she still worships, describes them as 'epic poems'. Each runs to hundreds of verses, in which she has evoked the lives of her father and his close friend, Dick Sheppard, the 'radio padre'. The room is piled high with her research papers, so much so that when I ask if she still listens to the wireless nowadays, she and I have to search through the mountains of paper to find her radio. In this room, she somehow managed to fit a BBC film crew when they came to interview her about Dick Sheppard for *Songs of Praise*.

This is a very quiet room, and Patricia adds to the atmosphere of calm and quiet in her being. Every week the room becomes even quieter (if possible), when Patricia welcomes the other nearby residents who belong to the Julian prayer group. This is one of many groups that meet for prayer and contemplation, inspired by the life of Mother Julian of Norwich, the fourteenth-century mystic.

They begin by listening to a reading, often from Julian's own *Revelations of Divine Love*, and then a little bell is rung. Patricia thinks that this bell was once used to summon the maid at the rectory of St Martin's. Now, it marks the beginning of thirty minutes of silence. Patricia begins by trying to repeat the Jesus Prayer. This prayer comes from the Orthodox Church, from the writings called the *Philokalia*, which translates as 'love of what is beautiful'. Repetition is an essential part of saying this prayer, and the Orthodox believer often looks at an icon of Christ as they pray the words. She says the prayer in her head, slowly and repeatedly, concentrating on Jesus, making space in her heart for his presence and love.

Lord Jesus Christ, Son of God,
Be merciful to me, a sinner.
The Jesus Prayer

Patricia has to try to clear her mind of all other thoughts, or the bell will sound to mark the end of the silence before she has even begun. She says she finds it very hard. With the wheeling seagulls calling for bread outside the window, and the sound of branches tapping gently on her window, it is very easy to be distracted. Patricia is not alone. She is in the distinguished company of a seventeenth-century dean of St Paul's and a twentieth-century dean of Westminster Abbey. John Donne, the poet and one of the most famous deans of St Paul's Cathedral, described his difficulties with prayer in a sermon:

I throwe myselfe down in my chamber, and I call God in, and invite God and his angels thither, and when they are there, I neglect God and his Angels, for the noise of a flie, for the rattling of a coach, for the whining of a doore; I talk on... eyes lifted up; knees bowed downe; as though I prayed to God; and if God or his Angels should ask me, when I last thought of God in that prayer, I cannot tell...

John Donne sermon (1626)

I was introduced to Donne's wonderful sermon by the Very Revd Michael Mayne, in a book that he finished writing shortly before he died. Michael was head of religious broadcasting in radio before he went on to greater things and became Dean of Westminster. He never forgot his broadcasting colleagues, and he and I used to meet in his medieval room in the deanery. There could not have been a more striking contrast with the austerity of his old BBC office, with its metal filing cabinets and tape recorders. Michael loved to show his guests how he could open an ancient lattice window in this room, not out onto the garden or the cloisters, but into the nave of the abbey. If the organ was being played then he and I would sometimes sit in the stillness of the room and just listen. None of the noisy distractions created by the thousands of visitors milling about the nave reached our sanctuary high above their heads.

Michael spent a lot of time alone in that room praying for those visitors, and for the world, to the God in whom he believed, and about whom he wrote so movingly in the last year of his life. He said that he knew that he could not pray 'Thy Kingdom come' unless he gave God space in his life. He had previously had ME, a debilitating disease that can be a very lonely experience since some people do not believe that it is even a real illness. Now he knew that his cancer was real, and fatal.

In the diary that makes up his book *The Enduring Melody*, Michael described the daily battle to concentrate on his prayers as his health worsened. He identified more and more with the seventeenth-century Dean of St Paul's as John Donne continued with his litany of distractions:

A memory of yesterday's pleasures, a fear of tomorrow's dangers, a straw under my knee, a noise in mine ear, an anything, a nothing, a fancy...

Michael writes how prayers could not be heard 'if we can't still our minds for long enough to give God a chance to speak'. He continues:

When my mind takes off, I say to God:
Loving Father, Source and end of my life, you know me infinitely better than I shall ever know myself; there is within me that which lies deeper than these trivial and inadequate words and random thoughts. Do not look on what I am but on what in my heart I desire to be...

Typically, for Michael was always free from all pomposity, he added, 'Or words to that effect.'

This is the first verse of Michael's favourite hymn:

O Thou who camest from above,
the pure celestial fire to impart,
kindle a flame of sacred love
on the mean altar of my heart
from 'O Thou who camest from above' by Charles Wesley (1707–88)

Blessings

• • • • • • • • • • • • •

*On the whole wide world
and God bless us every one*

*The Lord spoke to Moses, saying: 'Speak to Aaron and his sons, saying, "Thus
you shall bless the Israelites..."'*
Numbers 6:22–23

It was a familiar enough image for a religious programme: a man holding
forth in a pulpit, an open Bible on the lectern. But this was no ordinary
man and no ordinary holding forth. This was 'Daddy' King, pastor of
Ebenezer Baptist Church, Atlanta, Georgia, father of Martin Luther King,
Jr. He was about to pronounce a blessing as it had never before been seen
or heard on a television programme. Daddy King, as Martin Luther King,
Sr was always known, was the subject of one of the films that came closest
to what I had hoped to achieve during the time that I was editor of BBC's
religious documentary series, *Everyman*.

Daddy King had an extraordinary life. Like his famous son, who won
the Nobel Peace Prize for his campaign for civil rights, Daddy King fought
for justice for black people. Father and son shared the pulpit of Ebenezer
Baptist Church, and when his son was assassinated in 1968, Daddy King
took over his work.

By the time *Everyman* filmed him, Daddy King's wife, Alberta, had been
murdered too. At eighty-four, this huge, boomingly assertive man, whose
Christian faith was so formidable that he had renamed both himself and

his son 'Martin Luther' after the great reformer, was still captivating the congregations that he led in worship. Right at the end of the film the producer, Daniel Wolf, set the scene in a pulpit. Daddy King seemed to swell up and fill the space around him as he raised his hands high above his head, and in the words the Lord gave to Moses for Aaron, he seemed to bless the whole world:

The Lord bless you and keep you;
the Lord make his face to shine upon you
and be gracious to you;
the Lord lift up his countenance upon you
and give you peace.
Numbers 6:24–26

As I watched the first edit with Daniel on a wet weekday afternoon, Daddy King's voice seemed to encompass the deepest rumblings, which might have come from the centre of the earth, up to the highest pleading cry of an evolved man invoking the blessing of the God of Abraham and Isaac. Each phrase, separated by a dramatic pause, built on the last phrase until the final 'Amen' – which seemed like the resounding echo of all the prophets down the ages. Then his hands slowly dropped, as if he had released every ounce of energy and faith in his old body.

I have played the tape of this moment many times to many different people. Even sceptics and cynics who would normally avoid 'religious' broadcasting with disdain find themselves fascinated and disturbed by it. He himself is long dead, but Daddy King's blessing has not lost its fire.

———

In Rome there is another man whose prayers reach out to the whole world. On BBC One on Easter Day he speaks in sixty different languages, because by long tradition Pope Benedict XVI, 265th successor to Peter, delivers his annual blessing *Urbi et Orbi* – 'to the city and to the world'.

Easter was still two weeks away when our small delegation, representing all the British churches, assembled at dawn in St Peter's Square for the Papal Audience. Springtime in Rome had offered us hail, thunder and lightning and finally snow, but on the morning when Pope Benedict was to come out to greet visitors to the Eternal City it was bright and sunny.

Our party of Presbyterians, Baptists, Methodists, Anglicans and one Roman Catholic had to form a crocodile, clutching on to each other's coat tails as we pushed through the early morning crowds, as only one of us (no prizes for guessing who) had the admission card. We passed through one barrier after another and were even saluted by the Vatican's Swiss Guard in their medieval uniforms, standing ready to protect the Pontiff. Eventually we found our places in the second row, facing a chair that was not much smarter than the small plastic seats we were in. Gradually the row in front of us filled up with a mixed collection of people who were going to be personally presented to the Pope. Among them was a very wide nun, a huge man with a red fez on his head and a man carrying a large box, which later turned out to be a gift so heavy it almost felled the Holy Father.

After waiting for nearly two hours, the huge crowd behind us started to cheer, and suddenly, there he was, just a few feet away, careering up the slope to our level, riding in a white, open-topped jeep. As I watched him pass through my camera lens, he seemed to look straight at me and wave. Of course, naturally he would offer a personal greeting to our little ecumenical outpost from far-away Scotland, I thought... As it happens, when the film was processed, the photograph showed that he is looking straight at me, and I am left with the strong impression that he was saying to me, 'Oh, *you're* here. Now, what are we all going to do?'

The Papal Audience always concludes with a blessing, but before that the crowd is introduced to the Pope. From many countries of the world, and in eight different languages, we were announced in lists as long as a telephone directory. Each name met with a cheery wave from the formerly severe Cardinal Ratzinger, and those who made the most noise got the biggest wave and a huge smile that lit up his face like the sun coming out. Some people had more to offer than cheering: they sang songs and played musical instruments with wild abandon and great inaccuracy. The Pope sat through military marches, songs from the Russian steppes and several other cacophonies that would not make a parish talent contest. Every time they stopped, he gestured 'thank you', and seemed to mean it.

We all said the Lord's Prayer in our own language, and then he gave God's blessing to all of us but also, as he had just told us in English, to all those we loved – our families, friends and especially those we knew who were sick or anxious. As this slight figure in white stood up – not surrounded by the exotically garbed assistants I had expected and seeming quite vulnerable – all he said was:

May almighty God bless you,
The father, and the Son, and the Holy Spirit.

Suddenly, St Peter's Square seemed to be filled with friends and families. As we called out 'Amen', the whole world was mysteriously present in a simple and holy moment.

I bind unto myself today
The strong name of the Trinity,
By invocation of the same,
The three in one, and One in three,
Of whom all nature hath creation,
Eternal Father, Spirit, Word.
Praise to the Lord of my salvation:
Salvation is of Christ the Lord.
St Patrick (AD 372–466)

James Jones is the current Bishop of Liverpool. He has always taken an interest in religious broadcasting, and is often heard on Radio 2's *Pause for Thought* and Radio 4's *Thought for the Day*. He was the Church of England Bishop who, taking part in a series about Holy Week in the city, was prepared to find out about nightclub life by experiencing it for himself rather than judging it from the safe distance of his cathedral pulpit. He has frequently said that there is no room for comfortable complacency while every day the news brings us stories of the persistence of slavery all over the world. The blessing that he composed, and which he included in a Radio 4 service commemorating the 200th anniversary of William Wilberforce's parliamentary bill to abolish slave-trading, encourages everyone to go out into a world that will always need help:

> *May the Fire of Christ consume all indifference to God,*
> *The Light of Christ illumine our vision of God,*
> *The love of Christ enlarge our longing for God,*
> *And the Spirit of Christ empower our Service to God.*
> *And the Blessing of God Almighty,*
> *Father, Son and Holy Spirit,*
> *Be among us and remain with us always. Amen*
> **from 'The Liverpool Prayer 'James Jones, Anglican Bishop of Liverpool**

For many years *Songs of Praise* would end with a liturgical blessing on everyone watching by one of the clergy who had brought the different churches together for the hymn singing. These days the prayers at the end are said in different ways, often more personally, by different members of the congregation whose stories have been told during the programme. At other times the blessing is simply done by the final verse of a hymn, a 'doxology', in which God the Father who created us, God the Son who saved us, and God the Holy Spirit who sustains us, blesses us. This is Bishop Ken's final verse of 'Glory to thee, my God, this night for all the blessings of the light':

Praise God, from whom all blessings flow;
Praise him, all creatures here below;
Praise him above, ye heavenly host;
Praise Father, Son, and Holy Ghost. Amen
Thomas Ken (1637–1711)

One of the earliest radio broadcasts on New Year's Eve from the BBC's first headquarters in Savoy Hill ended with a sort of 'blessing' called 'The Grand Goodnight'. The announcer wished all the people he could think of 'good night'. They were not personally named, but he would mention the night workers sorting the mail, and all those who had come to the end of a hard year's work – the miners, farmers, street sweepers and lighthouse-keepers. It somehow united the whole nation in a benevolent gesture of goodwill from the BBC.

… Now music's prison'd rapture and the drown'd voice of truth
mantled in light's velocity, over land and sea
are omnipresent, speaking aloud to every ear,
into every heart and home their unhinder'd message,
the body and soul of Universal Brotherhood…
from 'The Testament of Beauty' by Robert Bridges (1844–1930)

It does not take a pope, a prelate, a pastor or even a hymn to offer God's blessing. We can all pray for God's blessing for someone we care about. Dorothy, a faithful and dedicated supporter of *Songs of Praise*, regularly phones me to exchange opinions about recent programmes. When it is time to ring off, she always ends with a cascade of blessings for everyone we have mentioned: the presenters, the producers and the members of the *Songs of Praise* office team. The ones she speaks to are in her prayers every day.

On a warm, sunny London afternoon in the late summer of 1973, I received the most important blessing of my life, and for the very first time I prayed my own. My mother, who had only just become an old-age pensioner, was at home lying in bed in the family drawing room. That lunchtime, she had finally admitted to us that she was dying. The doctor stood by her bed as he told my father, my brother and me. She had smiled gently, looking at us, but said nothing. She knew that we knew. It was typical of her not to express sadness or regret.

I had become used to her courage – too used to it really. Her cancer had lasted ten years. My brother had borne the burden of her everyday care for several months while I was far away in Scotland producing *Songs of Praise*, and when we spoke on the telephone she was so full of pride, having seen my name credit on the screen, that she did not talk about her health. Somehow, after so many false alarms, I had reverted, as all people perhaps do, to thinking that she was immortal.

Later that afternoon, I slipped in to see her again. She was lying down. Beside her was one of our old teddy bears, which she called Dr Orange. She had fallen into a coma, and her breathing was noisy. I sat and remembered how many parties she had organized in that room. I looked up at the picture rail where she used to balance holly on Christmas Eve, and at her writing desk, where I now sit as I write. It was the greatest treat when the desk was opened and we were allowed to get out all the family photos, especially the ones of her childhood and her wedding to my father, when the photographer had supplied all sorts of pictures of people that my parents claimed never to have met. She looked shy and vulnerable in her round glasses.

Suddenly, I had to rush out into the garden. Surrounded by the early evening singing of the many birds she used to feed, in a primal scream I mouthed 'It's unfair.' So much suffering in silence for her, and in a house where we never mentioned religion, where no questions were asked or answered. I felt as if I had erupted like a volcano. The birds continued to sing.

We seem to give them back to you, O God who gave them to us.
Yet as we did not lose them in giving, so we do not lose them in return.

Not as the world gives, do you give, O Lover of souls.
What you give you do not take away,
For what is yours is ours also if we are yours.
And life is eternal and love immortal, and death is only an horizon,
And an horizon is nothing save the limit of our sight.
Lift us up, strong Son of God, that we may see further;
Cleanse our eyes that we may see more clearly;
Draw us closer to yourself
That we may know ourselves to be nearer to our loved ones
Who are with you.
Animi Christi, from *St Benedict's Prayer Book* (1993)

I do not know whether she heard my strange outburst, but I went in, and acting completely out of character, took her hands and said 'God bless you'. Never, ever before had we held hands except in mutual embarrassment for 'Auld lang syne'. Now she gripped and squeezed my hand fiercely and tightly, and held on for a minute until her strength failed. Yet I felt deeply reassured, calmed, loved and blessed. 'No, Andy, it is not unfair,' I sensed she wanted me to know. 'This is life.'

On our heads and on our houses,
The Blessing of God.
In our coming and our going,
The Peace of God.
In our life and our believing,
The Love of God,
At our end and new beginning,
The arms of God to welcome us and bring us home.
Amen.
The Iona Community

Praying for Others

• • • • • • • • • • • • • •

Lotus flowers and St Pixel's

I have just hung up; why did he telephone?
I don't know… Oh! I get it…
I talked a lot and listened very little.

Forgive me, Lord, it was a monologue and not a dialogue.

I explained my idea and did not get his;
Since I didn't listen, I learned nothing,
Since I didn't listen, I didn't help,
Since I didn't listen, we didn't communicate.

Forgive me, Lord, for we were connected,
And now we are cut off.
from *Prayers of Life* (1965) by Michel Quoist

Michel Quoist's original prayer from the 1970s takes me back thirty years to the time when a new generation of religious broadcasters and producers arrived at the BBC. Many came straight from university, and it was a time of experiment and innovation in the world of religious ideas, as well as for new ways of approaching radio and television. The most original ideas would come from Peter Armstrong. An Oxford graduate new to the BBC's religious broadcasting department, Peter Armstrong entered a world that he found very puzzling. Religious television seemed to record people speaking, but not praying, in endless studio-based programmes in which the only visual feature to accompany the everlasting talking was a bunch of flowers from the local Shepherds Bush florist.

Peter knew Simon Tugwell, a young Dominican priest now living and working in Rome. In the early 1970s, the young Fr Simon was going through a 'hippy' phase; he would be found in London's Kings Road, sitting in cafés absorbed in discussions about new and unconventional spirituality. Peter asked the BBC One controller to let him make an experimental programme with Simon Tugwell, in which a flower would be used not as a decoration, but as a focus for meditation. Simon and two friends would sit in a circle in silence and pray. Viewers at home would be encouraged to do the same, as Peter directed shots both of the still and silent group, and of a single lotus flower in a bowl of water. Permission was unenthusiastically granted.

The full studio resources of four cameras and a vision and sound crew assembled as usual and asked for a script. 'There is none,' Peter had to keep repeating, as he explained that once everyone was in place, the normally frenzied operation of sound and cameramen moving about trying to remain out of shot would be unnecessary. All that the technicians had to do was point the cameras, and then keep still and silent. The sound engineer might perhaps pick up the quiet rhythm of breathing as the three people sat in a circle without moving a muscle. The crew looked as if they thought that this was some sort of hoax. Surely something was supposed to *happen* in a programme – even if it was 'just religion'?

It was one of the strangest, the quietest and the most powerful twenty minutes ever broadcast on the BBC. In the production gallery the normally shrilling telephones and excited instructions were all suspended. With scarcely a whisper, Peter slowly switched from one shot to another. Nobody spoke. Never had a lotus flower been so closely studied on television. Towards the end there was a little action: Peter murmured to the floor manager, 'Very quietly and gently, please replace the lotus flower with a rose and a crown of barbed wire.'

I am not sure that the second image, with its more obviously Christian imagery, made much difference, for we had already discovered that in our hectic lives, from our different religious upbringings, we were all sharing the same space and time for quiet thought and prayer. Something *did* 'happen' to everyone present. And it was clear that everyone was surprised and affected by the experience. Not surprisingly, the programme won an award at an international television festival.

> *O God of many names,*
> *Lover of all nations,*
> *We pray for peace*
> *In our hearts,*
> *In our homes,*
> *In our nations,*
> *In our world,*
> *The peace of your will,*
> *The peace of our need.*
> **Bishop George Appleton**

In 1977 Peter Armstrong found the money and persuaded the *Songs of Praise* team to introduce into the programme filmed interviews in which the local community would talk about their faith and choose the hymns. In 1979 he launched the documentary series *Everyman*, and then began to think about an entirely new way of helping people to worship together through television. Like all the most effective ideas for broadcasting, the programme would be very simple.

Peter, working with the late R.T. (Peter) Brooks and Liz, my wife, who had joined the department to be the first researcher for the new style *Songs of Praise* in 1977, began to think about how to make televised 'worship' more effective than simply doing an outside broadcast from a church. If you watched a drama on television, Peter reasoned, you were not shown shots of the audience sitting in the theatre, or made to watch it from behind a proscenium arch. Plays on television were especially designed for what television could do best – involve you intimately with the action. Could a television 'liturgy' be created that could really involve the viewers? What were the natural impulses that might lead people to worship, not from duty but from need? What were the sights and sounds of people's normal experience at home every Sunday? Did they in any way mirror the patterns of a church service?

There would be no hymn singing, no stained glass windows, crosses, icons or church spires. In *This is the Day*, viewers would see only everyday images that they could find all around them: the milk delivery, newspapers, suburban streets, cityscapes, seascapes, curtained windows, rubbish blowing down a street, gardens, television screens, radio aerials, taxis, shoppers, down and outs, photographs and headlines from newspapers.

It would begin with changing images of the dawn of a new day and, just as a church liturgy does, a prayer of thankfulness, followed by a time for remembering the things we wish we had done better – confession.

> *Bring us from the unreal to the real*
> *from despair to hope*
> *from darkness to light*
> *from death to eternal life.*
> **Angela Tilby, prayer used after 'confession' on *This is the Day***

The programme would be transmitted 'live' by satellite on Sunday mornings, and each week it would come from a different viewer's own home. People all around Britain would become the 'viewing congregation', and like the home the programme was coming from, they would be asked to have a flower, or light a candle, in front of their own television screen, and to have a Bible and some bread ready. There would be a Bible reading, followed by a meditation and time for silence. Viewers would write in, sharing their troubles and prayers for each other, and their letters would be read out and shown. Then, images from that morning's newspapers would be shown as the television audience prayed together for the world. Finally, viewers would be asked to break bread together.

Simple as an idea it may have been – and on the screen it had a very attractive simplicity – behind the scenes Liz and the crew had to mount a most complicated 'live' broadcast from a different front room every week. Huge amounts of apparatus, including a satellite dish, and a crew of twenty people from the BBC would be rushing hectically in and around a house in a quiet suburban street, as they set about creating 'an atmosphere of stillness', in which hundreds of thousands of people could pray for each other as they watched their televisions.

Perhaps the letter reading was the most moving part of the programme. Children and grandparents would ask for prayers for each other. People who were ill and waiting to go into hospital asked for prayers. Sometimes sick family pets would be offered up for healing. Others told stories of their fight with drug or alcohol addiction, or their fear of unemployment. As Liz opened the post every week, she looked too for the people who were thankful for an unexpected blessing, or simply wanted to celebrate life!

After the letters, everyone was asked to say a simple prayer:

The peace of Christ enfold us,
the love of Christ renew us,
the joy of Christ direct us,
now and for ever.

Each week, as the programme ended, the pictures showed the world preparing for the week ahead, as the final prayer was shared in every home:

Stand by us Lord,
Give us peace, courage and bright hopes,
this day and all our days.
Angela Tilby, closing prayer on *This is the Day*

This is the Day was shown for more than ten years, and in that time thousands of people wrote to ask for prayers, and prayed for the unseen others who they knew were watching too. One of the series producers was Angela Tilby, often heard today on *Thought for the Day* on Radio 4, and one of the earliest viewers to take part was a young student called Hugh Faupel, now the editor of *Songs of Praise* and television worship.

This is the Day is no longer shown (although it was apparently so simple it was also extremely expensive), but another original idea of Peter Armstrong's from as early as 1972 has been developed recently, and could turn out to be a very inexpensive and effective way of helping people all over the world to pray together.

Long before the first personal computer appeared (which was from the BBC, twenty-five years ago), using all sorts of special sound effects, Peter created a version of what it might be like if listeners could actually interact electronically with each other in worship – without leaving their homes. He had a priest to help him, Revd Roy Trevivian, who was as prepared to take risks in broadcasting as Dick Sheppard had been fifty years earlier. Every listener would have a microphone as well as a loudspeaker. This version, done with actors, had people hearing each other singing, and a worship leader who encouraged them to join in: 'Come on, you men!' he shouted. 'You can do better than that!' The resulting radio programme raised the blood pressure of many clergymen, but in those days it seemed about as likely to become a reality as a man landing on Mars.

Thirty-five years later, and enter St Pixel's, the first 'virtual' church. You go to your computer, type in 'St Pixel's' and join with whoever else is 'logged-on'. Every night at 9 p.m. people from all over the world come together at their keyboards and type in their prayers for each other and for themselves. Just by pressing the 'return' key, your prayer will appear on everyone else's screen. Each Friday night at 9.30 p.m. there is also a Bible study.

When BBC Radio 4's *Sunday Worship* featured St Pixel's in April 2007, some of the 'virtual' congregation became a real congregation at Emmanuel Church, Didsbury, home of the *Daily Service*. So why, asked Andrew Graystone, the presenter, would people prefer worshipping through their computer at home rather than going to church? One reason is that many people work seven days a week, and worship in the evening is all that they can manage. One such person working a seven-day week runs a Christian retreat centre. Another who has joined St Pixel's lives in the USA, so it is clear that the world is coming together through this 'virtual' church. Some of the participants suggested that Paul, who undertook his great journeys to spread the word, would have been able to make very good use of St Pixel's.

> *Father, hear the prayer we offer;*
> *Not for ease that prayer shall be,*
> *But for strength that we may ever*
> *Live our lives courageously*
> **Love Maria Willis (1824–1908)**

Prayer and Hope

● ● ● ● ● ● ● ● ● ● ● ● ●

Remembering Ian Mackenzie

A miracle is not when the impossible becomes possible, but when the impossible remains impossible and yet somehow happens.
from a sermon by Ian Mackenzie

Ian Mackenzie was a filmmaker who believed that prayer was not limited to words. It could be created from stone, water and all the elements of creation, and even from discarded frames of film on the editor's cutting bench. He was one of very few people who both produced *Songs of Praise* and appeared on it. He brought to the programme a personality that combined a great love and knowledge of music, enjoyment of television and film, and sometimes pure and unrivalled eccentricity. Johnston McKay, one of his producers, described him as 'the most creative and imaginative Christian I have ever met'.

Ian once said of making music, 'Few towns, villages, or city communities lack somebody who blows, scrapes, scratches, or hits things which make sounds.' As a very young assistant organist, but an already brilliant musician, he played the great organ of St Giles' Cathedral as an also very young Queen Elizabeth entered the building in 1953. He chose an improvisation on the tune 'She'll be coming round the mountain when she comes' as his extraordinary welcoming voluntary, played with such virtuosity that no one complained. We will never know if the monarch appreciated this unstuffy welcome to the heart of Scottish Presbyterianism.

He had a passion for arranging *Songs of Praise* to come from out-of-the-way places in Scotland, where local traditions were still alive. This included the haunting but very strange sound of 'lined' psalms sung in Gaelic, from the appropriately named community of Tongue. Each individual in the congregation, inspired by the Holy Spirit, lets their voice improvise around one note as they sing each line. Although rooted in the Psalms, it bears some resemblance to the Muslim call to prayer that sounds out from mosques five times a day. Another innovation that was not to be repeated was Ian's desire that *Songs of Praise* viewers should have a more familiar experience of attending church. Why should every pew be filled? And, instead of showing the singers' faces, why not use just one camera, situated right at the back, to get the visitors' normal view? Neither programme went down well in the southern suburban heartlands.

As a musician and a preacher who was knowledgeable about hymns, he had some individual insights. Ian maintained that the metrical version of Psalm 100, 'All People that on Earth do Dwell', should not be sung slowly, as it always is, but as the persecuted covenanters of the seventeenth century sang it – a lively celebration, each verse in just one big breath.

Ian Mackenzie was born a son of the manse and grew up in country and town parishes in Scotland and Prague, watching his father, as he described, 'make the pulpit sing'. Although an ordained minister in the Church of Scotland, he became an ITV producer in London, and then head of religious broadcasting for BBC Scotland for sixteen years. In 1989 he retired from the BBC after a heart attack.

> *Lord, now lettest thou thy servant depart in peace: according to thy word.*
> *For mine eyes have seen thy salvation,*
> *Which thou hast prepared: before the face of all people;*
> *To be a light to lighten the Gentiles: and to be the glory of thy people*
>   *Israel.*

Glory be to the Father, and to the Son: and to the Holy Spirit;
As it was in the beginning, is now, and ever shall be; world without end.
Amen

Nunc Dimittis (Luke 2:29–32), from the Service of Evensong, *The Book of Common Prayer* (1662)

Knowing him to be a lover of English Cathedral Evensong, even though a Presbyterian minister, I called for Ian's help in one of my own last *Songs of Praise* programmes, which was to come from his home church in Helensburgh. One sequence was to remember the lives of all submariners lost at sea. Ian helped produce and arrange the music to go over the filmed images: a solo trumpeter from the Royal Marines playing Geoffrey Burgon's version of the *Nunc Dimittis*, well known because it had been sung week by week at the end of each episode of the BBC dramatization of John le Carré's *Tinker, Taylor, Soldier, Spy*. The trumpeter was nervous, but Ian, arriving in his ancient anorak, coaxed a beautiful and moving performance out of him. Before we could say 'thank you', he was gone: a man who found praise and 'gush' hard to take. But if Ian's work with the Gaelic psalm singers had not been a national hit, this certainly was.

Listeners loved his radio broadcasts, and before answering the many letters that always followed, he could only bear to listen to the recording of his own programmes when sitting in his car, on his own, looking at the lochs and mountains of the western Highlands.

Liz and I loved his letters, especially at Christmas. No round robin about family triumphs on the cricket field, these letters shared life with all its woes and wonders from the point of view of one or other of the family pets, and even the battered family car. A bath Ian was taking was described as 'enormous, steamy and profound' and Donald, a friend's dog, as 'currently deceased'. They ended in Ian's own weird spidery hand, with sentences creeping up the side of the page.

In the very last service he broadcast on Radio 4, he used a prayer that had come to him in just a minute in the middle of a sleepless night:

O Thou whom I meet in the fears that bank up on the horizon,
Calm me.
O Thou whom I meet in the tears that flood the horizon,
Navigate me.
O Thou whom I meet in the years that have carried me over the horizon,
Keep me moving.
O Thou whom I shall meet when my end nears,
Take me.
O Thou, Creator, Redeemer, Spirit, whom I have met in the circle of
  infinity,
Complete me.
Ian Mackenzie, musician, preacher and broadcaster (1931–2006)

Ian died suddenly in October 2006. May Ian, and all those we have loved and will see no more:

Rest in peace
and rise in Glory.

When dark despair is all around,
And falling tears the only sound,
Light one small flame of hope that still
You walk with us, and always will.
Enfold in love for ever more
All those we love, but see no more.
from 'O Father, on your love we call' by Jean Holloway

Prayer for the Future

· · · · · · · · · · · · · ·

Lord, for tomorrow

Lord, for tomorrow and its needs,
I do not pray;
But keep me, guide me, love me, Lord,
Just for today.
Sister M Xavier (1856–1917)

This hymn, which is also a prayer, has often been chosen for *Songs of Praise*. Sometimes it has helped someone who is coping day by day with chronic illness, or worse, waiting for news about the health of someone they love. This has happened several times in my own life. My impatience always gets to work, so that I become like a mad sheriff in the Wild West, wanting to gather up a 'posse' to ride along with me and 'fix' the problem.

The kind family doctor around the corner, who once offered immediate calm and reassurance, has largely been replaced by the less personal 'group practice', and by hospital tests with hi-tech machinery, which we then have to wait in a long queue for a clever but unknown 'specialist' to decode before anyone explains what might be the cause of our symptoms. There is always a lot of waiting, of feeling completely powerless, and all sorts of anxieties fill up the long hours. But patience in adverse circumstances has always been a great and hard-won virtue.

God, give us grace to accept with serenity
the things we cannot change,
courage to change the things we must,
and the wisdom to know the difference.
Reinhold Niebuhr (1882–1971)

In the last days of 1999 everyone who had a computer, whether the sort that has helped produce this book or one of the intricate machines that controls the world's money or helps test our bodies, became very anxious for 'tomorrow'. It was for the oddest and simplest of reasons: would every computer everywhere in the world shut down in confusion when the date 1999 was replaced by 2000? Within the millions of numbers that make up any computer program (even including a digital watch), registering the date and time is crucial. It seemed that it was a distinct possibility that none of our computers would recognize a year that did not begin '19xx'. We all began to fear the millennium 'bug'.

The BBC's religious broadcasters were as anxious as anyone. They had prepared an extra-special 'Auld lang syne' to be sung at midnight, but would the machines that play each *Songs of Praise* programme through the transmitters, and even all the power stations themselves, suddenly switch off? Would we be saying 'Happy New Millennium' to each other in a dark, silent world?

There was nothing at all that programme-makers could do while hundreds of boffins argued and pondered the issue, then descended on every device that needed to be instructed that 2000 was not a signal to switch off. Along with television colleagues in Wales and Ireland, BBC Scotland had persuaded the programme planners to allow us to unite young people in all three nations and broadcast them saying a prayer together for the future. It would happen in the final few minutes before midnight, as we said farewell to a thousand years of British history that stretched back beyond the Battle of Hastings.

I suggested that they read the Beatitudes, the promise of future blessings that Jesus made to his followers in his Sermon on the Mount. These words, broadcast 'live' from several different beautiful places in our islands, including the tiny chapel of St Margaret in the ancient heart of Edinburgh Castle, would speak to the anxious and offer hope. It might even distract them from worrying about their digital clocks.

Then midnight struck – and we all know what happened next.

Blessed are the poor in spirit,
for theirs is the kingdom of heaven.
Blessed are those who mourn,
for they will be comforted.
Blessed are the meek,
for they will inherit the earth.
Blessed are those who hunger and thirst for righteousness,
for they will be filled.
Blessed are the merciful,
for they will receive mercy.
Blessed are the pure in heart,
for they will see God.
Blessed are the peacemakers,
for they will be called children of God.
Blessed are those who are persecuted for righteousness' sake,
for theirs is the kingdom of heaven.
Blessed are you when people revile you and persecute you
and utter all kinds of evil against you falsely on my account.
Rejoice and be glad,
for your reward is great in heaven,
for in the same way they persecuted the prophets who were before you.
Matthew 5:3–12, spoken by young people from the three nations
at the dawn of the new millennium

Since the new millennium began, news broadcasts from all around the world have brought increasing reports of earthquakes, tsunamis, hurricanes and melting polar ice caps. Even while I have been writing this book, Scotland has been blooming in the most perfect spring. Almost as I watch from the window, blossoms multiply on the trees and plants spread across the recently bare winter garden. Although millions of us have been enjoying this unexpected and unusual warm sunshine, the media has been making even more dire predictions of global warming. The earth is heating up, the sea is rising, and not much further into the future – because of how we misuse the earth's resources – we will all perish.

A sense of guilt has always played a part in our relationship with nature. We are dependent for life on the creation, on the regular turning of the seasons; and from the earliest biblical accounts of the flood, we have feared the judgement of God when nature veers from its normal course. In the sixteenth century, when most people in Britain lived off the land and grew their own produce, if there was a drought, they prayed:

> *O God, who sendest rain upon the just and the unjust;*
> *We beseech thee that we being delivered from our offences, may receive*
> *abundantly, of thy bounty, the rain we have waited for,*
> *Whereby both health and nourishment may be granted to us.*
> **from The Sarum Missal**

When it rained, and rained, and rained, they would fear that God was sending a new flood to punish them, so they prayed:

> *O Lord, hear our prayer, and accept the vows of thy people;*
> *and bid the immoderate outpourings of rain to cease;*
> *and turn this scourge of the elements to the setting forth of thy mysteries,*
> *that they who rejoice to have been born again in the water of regeneration*

may also rejoice
in their correction by this chastisement.
from *The Sarum Missal*

There is no doubt that global warming is a real and present danger, and we must start to live in greater harmony with nature and the processes that have made this earth such a beautiful place for human life. It is urgent, but we need not feel completely helpless. Each individual response, as well as each political action, will make a difference. And we have the most powerful resource of all: we can pray. Everyone who takes part in the Week of Prayer for Christian Unity in the future will be asked to put their prayers into action in their daily lives.

Wars, too, continue to come into our homes through television, radio and even the computer, which was, of course, quite untroubled by the millennium date. In 2001 millions of us all over the world looked on in horror at the moment when the Twin Towers in New York collapsed, and thousands of people, from many different races and religions, died before our eyes.

The apocalyptic images of that day were played and replayed on our television screens. In the small Perthshire town of Pitlochry, the rector of the Episcopal church, remembering his own days of anxiety at war as a chaplain in the Royal Navy, travelled around speaking to shocked parishioners and tourists, and gave each of them a small card containing a simple prayer for the future:

Lord
Bring peace
Into
Your world.
The Revd Roger Devonshire, former chaplain to the Royal Navy

Just as I am, thou wilt receive,
Wilt welcome, pardon, cleanse, relieve:
Because thy promise I believe
O Lamb of God, I come.

from 'Just as I am, without one plea' by Charlotte Elliott (1789–1871)

Thanksgiving

● ● ● ● ● ● ● ● ● ● ● ● ● ●

Humble and hearty thanks

Now thank we all our God,
with hearts and hands and voices,
who wondrous things hath done,
in whom his world rejoices;
who from our mothers' arms
hath blessed us on our way
with countless gifts of love,
and still is ours today.
Martin Rinkart (1586–1649)

When I began producing *Songs of Praise* in the 1960s, I discovered – to
my surprise – that in every town and city of the British Isles members of
churches of all denominations, from extreme Protestant to ultra-Catholic,
however divided theologically or politically, were happy to unite to sing
hymns in front of the television cameras. But I also discovered an old
division based on which side a town's inhabitants had supported in the
seventeenth-century civil war, which could give some towns a very
different character from their neighbours. For example, churches in
Tunbridge Wells in Kent, a town that developed from a Cavalier meeting
place into a fashionable spa, are quite different in character from those in
neighbouring Tonbridge, a Roundhead town, where they still retain a
Puritan atmosphere.

It was in the aftermath of the Civil War, at the end of Oliver Cromwell's Commonwealth and during the difficult days of the Restoration, that one of Christianity's great prayers was written by a man, Edward Reynolds, who did much to help old enemies become friends:

Almighty God, Father of all mercies,
we thine unworthy servants do give thee
most humble and hearty thanks
for all thy goodness and loving-kindness to us, and to all men
(*particularly to those who desire now to offer up their praises and
thanksgivings for thy late mercies vouchsafed unto them).
We bless thee for our creation, preservation,
and all the blessings of this life;
but above all, for thine inestimable love in the redemption of the world by
our Lord Jesus Christ; for the means of grace and for the hope of glory.
And, we beseech thee, give us that due sense of all thy mercies, that our
hearts may be unfeignedly thankful, and that we shew forth thy praise,
not only with our lips, but in our lives;
By giving up ourselves to thy service,
and by walking before thee in holiness and righteousness all our days;
Through Jesus Christ our Lord,
to whom with thee and the Holy Ghost be all honour and glory,
world without end. Amen
The General Thanksgiving, from *The Book of Common Prayer* (1662)

The first moments of the Restoration of the monarchy, after years of civil war, seem to have been marked by farcical scenes of bowing and scraping on Dover beach. From contemporary accounts, it sounds like something from television's *Blackadder*. As the long-exiled King Charles II stepped ashore at Dover on a May afternoon a witness recorded, 'Now did all put themselves into a posture, for to observe the meeting of the best of kings and most deserving of subjects. The admirers of Majesty were jealous of too low a condescension, and the lovers of duty fearful on the other side of an ostentation of merit.' However, it is recorded that in the end 'all parties were satisfied'.

There were also carefully staged gestures of piety. The king had scarcely stepped ashore when Mr Reading, the Minister of Dover, presented him with a large Bible adorned with gold clasps. The next morning, Sunday 27 May, King Charles II arrived in Canterbury and 'went to his devotions to the Cathedral, which was very much dilapidated, yet the people seemed glad to hear the Common Prayer again'.

Charles II was not so much a devout person as a politically astute monarch. He had immediately acknowledged both the Bible, which the Puritans of the Commonwealth had promoted as the only proper basis for worship, and Edward VI's *Book of Common Prayer* of 1549, which had survived in secret, hidden by the handful of bishops who escaped the Lord Protector's purge. The returning monarch needed the loyalty of both Anglican bishops and Puritan ministers if he was to have any chance of governing the country.

Oliver Cromwell's last illness had been marked by depression and paranoia; he was surrounded by religious fanatics 'intoxicated by visionary absurdities and a lust for power'. His son who succeeded him said he would only trust a man who could neither pray nor preach. Even so, old Cavaliers warned Charles II that 'if there were not a minister in every parish, you would quickly find cause to increase the number of constables'. The balance of state power would only be restored with the return of an established church, the controlling influence of bishops and their appointed clergy, and the strict use of the authorized services of the prayer book.

One man, Edward Reynolds, although he had staunchly supported the Puritan cause and the abolition of bishops, saw that the times had changed, and agreed to become Bishop of Norwich and to work under the eye of the king to revise the 1549 prayer book alongside Robert Sanderson, another newly appointed bishop and a supporter of the Cavalier cause.

As Charles II made his royal progress through England, fêted by the most exotic displays of loyalty, all the clergy were encouraged to pray, 'May God preserve you in safety from domestic conspiracies, and so fasten you as a nail in a sure place.'

They had good reason to pray. A contemporary account described the emergence of 'wild barbarous men, the most desperate and bloody enthusiasts, fifth-monarchy-men that ever appeared in this or perhaps any other nation'.

Thomas Venner, by trade a cooper but also a self-elected preacher, assembled a well-armed gang at his meeting house in London on Sunday, 6 January 1661. Venner's mission was said to be 'to erect a fifth monarchy for the personal reign of Jesus Christ upon Earth. They would never sheath their swords, till Babylon, as they called monarchy, became a hissing and a curse.' After winning Britain, they would take France, Germany and Spain, since they believed that no weapon would even hurt a hair of their heads for 'one should chase a thousand, and two put ten thousand to flight'.

Fifth Monarchists believed in the imminent return of Jesus to rule the earth. Today some perfectly peace-loving Christians still pray in anticipation of this, but in the seventeenth century Venner and other preachers interpreted passages in the books of Daniel and Revelation as telling them to take up arms against the State, in order to bring about Christ's return. They marched to St Paul's churchyard and 'declared for King Jesus', killing a man who declared for King Charles. A horrible riot followed, during which an attempt was made to kidnap the lord mayor. Two other preachers were killed, as were twenty of the king's troops. The battle went as far as Hampstead Heath, where many of the Fifth Monarchists were killed. Venner himself died of wounds received in the final battle in a pub.

It all sounds rather trivial in a way, but strangely, it had a profound effect on England. There had been many similar plots to kill both Charles I and Oliver Cromwell, and memories of the Gunpowder Plot and Guy

Fawkes' attempt to blow up Parliament were still fresh in people's minds. 'Had their numbers been equal to their spirits, they would have subverted the City, the Kingdom and the World,' remarked one eyewitness.

Fortunately there were also men like Bishops Robert Sanderson and Edward Reynolds, the latter described by his biographer, Isaac Walton, as 'one who discerns things that differ exactly, passeth his judgement rationally and expresses it aptly, clearly and honestly'. A church expressed through reason, the Bible, and a book of common prayer for all to use would, Sanderson and Reynolds believed, bring an end to the 'dreadful commotions'.

Bishop Edward Reynolds became known for his meditations of comfort and healing, and he wrote the General Thanksgiving, which speaks more eloquently than any other prayer as to how we are all connected to God, each other and all creation.

———

I was not a grateful little boy, at least to judge by my memories of the words 'ungrateful child' frequently being uttered by elderly relatives. My brother and I grew up having to be reminded repeatedly that 'please is a very little word, and thank you is not long'. My mother, they said, was giving her life for my younger brother and me. But showing gratitude was something that just did not seem to come naturally to us. There had been few if any spontaneous demonstrations of gratitude before I was eleven, when my father reached into his office suit pocket on his return home one evening to produce a fountain pen for me. I instantly clasped him with joy and kissed him on his stubbly cheek. He looked astonished and a bit shocked, and I immediately reverted to my natural self-conscious self, scarcely making eye contact with the rest of the world.

I do not remember when I first heard the General Thanksgiving, but I am sure that I heard it before I read it. At school, it was said every night at some speed by the whole house assembled for prayers, but apart from the words 'humble and hearty', I could not make out what everyone was saying. I seemed to be the only boy who did not know this prayer by heart. Perhaps that is why on the fly-leaf of the prayer book that had been sent in my trunk with me to school I had written, 'Prep: look at General Thanksgiving'.

I gradually became more familiar with the words of this prayer, and could even join in when the congregation at home mumbled through it rather more slowly somewhere near the end of Mattins week by week in our parish church. 'Humble', I reckoned I could try for; 'hearty' was unimaginable. 'Hearty' described our cousins, immensely tall and immensely good at games. They were good because they were good at losing, I was told, although they never lost when I was playing with them.

My father often spoke of the thankfulness that silence and a long walk gave him, and on Sunday afternoons another ritual was inevitable. 'Who would like to go for a walk?' There were not many takers – just my father and his eldest son. It was another call of duty and certainly did not inspire humble and hearty thanks in me, who had already dutifully endured church, but my mother always hinted that my father would be lonely without a companion. He never said that; indeed, I have no memory of him saying much at all as we set off, beginning with a short dash along the pavement of our tarmac side road until we reached the place where the road was unsurfaced and the trees began. There we proceeded at a measured, unchanging pace around the course. It was always the same, and it was boring and without incident. Only the occasional car would pass us, almost at our walking pace, bucking and bouncing in the huge potholes.

We always made for a sort of woodland wilderness, circling and criss-crossing a maze of tracks, all marked out by wicket fences. Men in brown homburg hats and Harris Tweed suits policed visitors, causing my father to lift his hat or wave his walking stick in greeting. Then the click as his stick struck the stony path, and the swishing of fallen dead leaves as his young companion pretended to be a snowplough were all that broke the silence. I used to try to imagine what would happen if we suddenly found a steamroller at work, or a fire engine, or a giraffe.

Fifty years on, I returned to our old circuit. Miraculously, a few roads have still been left unsurfaced, and on a dry summer's day, clouds of dust engulf four-wheel drive cars shooting past, much less fearful of losing their suspension. Then silence falls. I do not remember so many birds singing in the old days, but the paths look familiar, the huge horse chestnuts in full flower unchanged. Only the fences and the brown-suited neighbours are gone. Even with no walking stick clattering just a pace or two ahead, I follow the same track without hesitation, honouring the old route. I wish that I could say thank you to the silent companion who introduced me to a place that now seems very beautiful.

Our walks continued for ten years or more. Most of that time, my mother was unobtrusively coping with cancer. Every two years, another operation was suddenly essential, and we all silently held our breath. She rarely joined us on the walk, but her life revolved around us. If my brother or I had a big exam to take or a holiday planned together, she would keep her latest symptoms to herself until our big day was past. She was grateful for every second that we spent together. We came first, and her health second.

Today, walking along our old paths, I now better understand 'humble and hearty thanks'. I imagine my father thinking of these words as he padded through this wilderness, where he would give his silent thanks for the 'creation, preservation and all the blessings of this life' he had shared with my mother. As we all inwardly tried to imagine the unimaginable – life without a wife and mother – he was struggling to pray, just as Bishop Reynolds had, emerging from the perils of plague and war in the seventeenth century, for 'that due sense of all thy mercies, that our hearts may be unfeignedly thankful'.

During all those years, we never spoke about prayer. It was not until near the end of his own life that I first even had a conversation with my father about the prayer book. He 'didn't care' (his strongest expression of disapproval) for the new books, and he had joined the Prayer Book Society. His old prayer book came to me when I collected his possessions from the hospital after he died. It was autographed by a famous headmaster of Rugby, W.W. Vaughan, on the day my father had been confirmed. On a particularly well-thumbed page are the words of the General Thanksgiving.

So to those words that I could not understand as I muddled through childhood trying to be good, I can now add, as I remember my mother and father and many other 'late mercies', just as the choir sings every week at the end of *Choral Evensong* on Radio 3, 'Thanks be to God'.

The Creed

● ● ● ● ● ● ● ● ● ● ● ● ●

I believe

Within a hundred years of the life of Christ, the newly formed church began to write down its statement of belief, using the creation of the world, and the birth, death and resurrection of Jesus as its manifesto. The wording of the earliest creed (from Latin *credo* – 'I believe') that has survived, possibly in use from AD 150, was accepted by all the Western Catholic churches, although not by the Orthodox churches of the East. By the fourth century it had become known as 'The Apostles' Creed', and although it is unlikely that the twelve apostles knew it in this form, the words are clearly derived from their original teaching and gospel thought.

From earliest times some form of the creed was to be said, as it still is today, by anyone coming forward for baptism. Anyone can baptize another person who has confessed their faith in the words of the creed by pouring water on to their forehead and, beginning with their name, saying, 'I baptize you in the name of the Father and the Son and the Holy Spirit'. Today, if a baby is to be baptized in the Anglican Church, the creed will be said on its behalf by the parents and godparents, joined by everyone else who has come to witness the newcomer being welcomed into the Christian family. This is an important moment that must only happen once in a person's life. Once they are baptized they have become, as the Anglican baptism service declares, 'Christ's own'.

St Mary's Episcopal Cathedral in Edinburgh was more than normally full one Sunday in the new year of 2007. Three very extended families had joined the regular congregation, and during the service we would witness the baptism of Holly, Monica and Isla. As each proud mother held her own daughter, the Revd Dean Fostekew, who had prepared the families for this moment, led them to the font and prayed over the water in words that told the story so far:

Holy God, well-spring of life,
in your love and justice,
you use the gift of water to declare your saving power.
In the beginning your Spirit moved over the face of the waters.
By the gentle dew, the steady rain,
you nourish and give increase to all that grows;
you make the desert a watered garden.
You command the wildness of the waves;
when the storm rages you calm our fear;
in the stillness you lead us to a deeper faith.
In the life-giving rivers and the rainbow
Israel discerned your mercy.
You divided the Red Sea
to let them pass from slavery in Egypt
to freedom in the Promised Land.
In the waters of Jordan
penitents found forgiveness in the baptism of John.
There, Jesus your beloved child
was anointed with the Holy Spirit,
that he might bring us
to the glorious liberty of the children of God.
Liturgy of Holy Baptism,
Scottish Episcopal Church 2006

None of the babies – in this case three of the quietest babies I can ever remember – were likely to remember the moment when gently warmed water was poured from a scallop shell on to their foreheads, but it was, I believe, the most important of their lives. The whole congregation joined in to pray that out of this present moment there would be a great future for Holly, Monica and Isla, and for all of us:

> *Bring those who are baptised in this water,*
> *with Christ through the waters of death,*
> *to be one with him in his resurrection.*
> *Sustain your people by your spirit*
> *to be hope and strength to the world.*
> **Liturgy of Holy Baptism,**
> **Scottish Episcopal Church 2006**

Suffering from a cough, which echoed horribly around the cathedral, and having already almost obliterated the opening hymn, I realized that I would have to keep my mouth shut for the creed. Far from being a rejection of the faith that we are all asked to declare, I found that hearing other people all around me say the words was like being introduced to something that I had never heard before, each phrase a new and extraordinary discovery:

> *I believe in God the Father almighty,*
> *maker of heaven and earth:*
> *and in Jesus Christ his only Son our Lord,*
> *who was conceived by the Holy Ghost,*
> *born of the Virgin Mary,*
> *suffered under Pontius Pilate,*
> *was crucified, dead and buried.*
> *He descended into hell;*
> *the third day he rose again from the dead;*

he ascended into heaven,
and sitteth on the right hand of God the Father almighty;
from thence he shall come to judge the quick and the dead.
I believe in the Holy Ghost;
the holy catholic Church;
the communion of saints;
the forgiveness of sins;
the resurrection of the body,
and the life everlasting.
Amen.

The Apostles' Creed, from *The Book of Common Prayer* (1662)

The creed is every Christian's story of liberation, not imprisonment. So I wonder why we in the congregation often sound so dreary and weary when we say it together. In an Anglican cathedral at Evensong, after a marvellous choir has sung the words of the *Nunc Dimittis* (Simeon's song of joy when he held the child, Jesus, in his arms) we dutifully turn to face the high altar at the east end if we are in the choir stalls, and begin to mutter like monotonous station announcers. We battle on to the end and the chance to sit down, completely missing the news of 'life everlasting'.

I think that if I lose my memory as I grow old, I would like this to be the last prayer that I do remember. One evening last summer, I was sitting with a group of priests as they finished a very long day of lecturing to a small group of men and women who were about to be ordained into the ministry of the Anglican Church. Having spent twenty-four hours with them, it was clear to me that they were a very talented bunch, eager and anxious to serve the community. But that night, in a particularly ill-lit room, they all seemed exhausted and apprehensive about the future, especially when they were told to break up into pairs and, in just a few minutes, write down a creed that expressed all that they believed about God and his call to them.

'Why don't you write one too?' the lecturer said to me as I was trying to remain invisible in a shadowy corner. Here, because people asked me for copies when I read it out, is what I wrote:

I believe in God
Who makes the impossible possible
But does not call me to do it instead:
Present in the darkness but who is making the dawn.

I believe in God
Who has in Jesus lived and died in failure;
Whose essence is forgiveness
And who forgives me now.

I believe in God, who is love,
Who has been, is now
And will be forever
Surprised and surprising.
A creed for the weary and disheartened by Andrew Barr

Text Acknowledgments

Every effort has been made to trace and acknowledge copyright holders of all the quotations included. We apologize for any errors or omissions that may remain, and would ask those concerned to contact the publishers, who will ensure that full acknowledgment is made in any reprint.

p. 8 Extract from 'I Wish I Knew How it Would Feel to be Free' by Billy Taylor and Richard Carroll Lamb. Permission granted by Westminster Music Ltd; p. 8–9 Extract from 'Before the World Began'. Words John L Bell and Graham Maule © 1987, WGRG, Iona Community G2 3DH; p. 12 Extract from *Under Milk Wood* by Dylan Thomas published by J M Dent & Sons, 1954. Permission granted by David Higham Associates; pp. 14, 23, 29, 32, 34, 41, 74, 88, 97, 122–23, 132, 142 Extracts from *The Book of Common Prayer*, the rights in which are vested in the Crown, are reproduced by permission for the Crown's Patentee, Cambridge University Press. Used with permission; p. 17–18 Extract from 'Slow Down My Lord' taken from *Short Prayers for the Long Day* by Giles and Melville Harcourt, published by Harper Collins, 1978; p. 20 Extract taken from *The Everlasting Mercy* by John Masefield. Permission granted by The Society of Authors as the Literary Representative of the Estate of John Masefield; p. 26 Permission granted by Revd Stephen Shipley; p. 30 Extract from 'Expectant' by Jim Cotter, taken from *Verses for Advent*, Cairns Publications 2002. Permission granted by Jim Cotter; pp. 31–33, Extracts from *The Book of Common Worship*, published by Church House Publishing, 2000; p. 35 Extract from 'Come Join the Celebration' by Valerie Collison published by Hi-Fye Music, 1972; p. 35 Extract from 'Lord Jesus, born in Bethlehem' by John Irvine, the Dean of Coventry. p. 38 Extract from 'The Butterfly Song' by Brian Howard. Permission granted by CopyCare; p. 40 Extract taken from the song 'Father God I wonder' by Ian Smale. Copyright © 1984 Thankyou Music. Adm. By worshiptogether.com songs excl. UK and & Europe, adm. By kingswaysongs.com tym@kingsway.co.uk. Used with permission; p. 43 Extract from 'I shall be sheltered in the shadow' translated by Archimandrite Ephrem Lash, taken from *An Orthodox Prayer Book* published by Oxford University Press, 1999; p. 52 Extract from 'We Have A Gospel to Proclaim' by Edward Burns. Permission granted by Edward Burns; p. 61 Prayer by Brother Roger of Taizé. © Ateliers et Presses de Taizé, 71250 Taizé, France; pp. 67 and 98 Prayer for the National Lent Course of 1986 and Prayer from an order of service (2005) for the churches of Britain and Ireland for Remembrance Sunday. Permission granted by Churches Together in Britain and Ireland; p. 69 'Lord God, whose son was content to die' by Dr Ian M Fraser. Permission granted by Dr Fraser; p. 70 'Holy Spirit, rushing, burning' by Stewart Cross. Permission granted by Mrs Mary Cross; pp. 86 and 87 Extracts from 'Longing for Light, We Wait in Darkness' by Bernadette Farrell. Used with permission; p. 78 Extract from 'God, Beyond Our Dreams' by Bernadette Farrell. Used with permission; p. 87 Extract from 'Bless, O God, those with hymns' by Norman Wallwork. Reproduced with the Permission of The Epworth Press and Revd Preb. Norman Wallwork. pp. 89, 90, 90–91, 91–92 Collects for Janani Luwum, Thomas Cranmer, Swithun and Hilda from *Exciting Holiness* 2nd edition, published by Canterbury Press Norwich 2003. Used with permission; p. 110 The Liverpool Blessing by James Jones, the Bishop of Liverpool. © James Jones. p. 113 'On our heads and on our houses' © WGRG, Iona Community, G2 3DH; p. 114 The poem 'The Telephone' by Michael Quoist from *Prayers of Life* is reproduced with the permission of the publishers Gill & Macmillan, Dublin; p. 116 'O God of many names' by George Appleton from *The Oxford Book of Prayer* published by Oxford University Press; p. 124 'O thou whom I meet in the fears' by Ian McKenzie. Permission granted by his estate; p. 124 Extract from 'O Father on your love we call' by Jean Holloway; p. 140–41 Liturgy of Holy Baptism, Scottish Episcopal Church. Used with permission of the Scottish Episcopal Church.